Kerala

David Stott

D0626336

Credits

Footprint credits
Editorial and production: Nicola Gibbs
Maps: Kevin Feeney

Publisher: Patrick Dawson
Managing Editor: Felicity Laughton
Advertising: Elizabeth Taylor
Sales and marketing: Kirsty Holmes

Photography credits

Front cover: Ajijchan / Dreamstime.com
Back cover: Zzvet / Dreamstime.com

Printed in Great Britain by alphaset, Surbiton

Every effort has been made to ensure that the facts in this guidebook are accurate. However, travellers should still obtain advice from consulates, airlines, etc, about travel and visa requirements before travelling. The authors and publishers cannot accept responsibility for any loss, injury or inconvenience however caused.

Publishing information
Footprint *Focus Kerala*
2nd edition edition
© Footprint Handbooks Ltd
April 2014

ISBN: 978 1 909268 79 1
CIP DATA: A catalogue record for this book is available from the British Library

® Footprint Handbooks and the Footprint mark are a registered trademark of Footprint Handbooks Ltd

Published by Footprint
6 Riverside Court
Lower Bristol Road
Bath BA2 3DZ, UK
T +44 (0)1225 469141
F +44 (0)1225 469461
footprinttravelguides.com

Distributed in the USA by Globe Pequot Press, Guilford, Connecticut

Contents

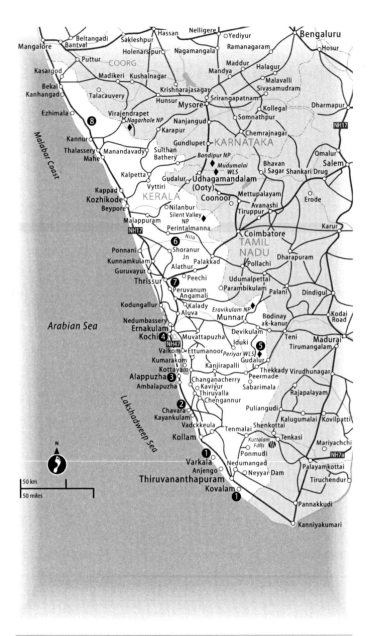

Kerala ebbs by at snail's pace, most picturesquely in the slow-flowing networks of lagoons and rivers that make up its backwaters, where nature grows in such overwhelming profusion that canals sit choked with pretty water-lily thickets and dragonflies bunch in clouds over lotus leaves. Dawn mists drift through canopies made by antique mango and teak trees, as farmers slip their oars into the silent waters, and women's dresses glare extra bright in the reflections of the still glass waters.

In the ramshackle port city of Fort Kochi, it's as if the clocks stopped a few centuries back: wizened traders sift spice in the shadows of derelict go-downs, the churches glow lime white, at the harbour's edge lines of cantilevered Chinese fishing nets swoop for their next catch of silvery sprats, and medieval streets and antique shops thread the route between the tiny blue-tiled synagogue and grand Dutch wooden palace of Mattancherry.

The southern beaches of Kovalam and Varkala are great places to unwind with Ayurvedic massages, but Malabar, in the north, is the real unsung jewel of the state, an outpost of staunch Hindu religiosity and capital of the Muslim Moplah community. Here, hushed families gather at dawn in leafy temple gardens to watch spectacles of the unique, hypnotic temple dance form *Theyyam* and, come nightfall, the precision athletes of the swashbuckling martial art *Kalarippayattu* draw their swords.

Switchback turns bear you from the lush green paddy fields of the plains through spindly rubber plantations and blooming coffee-tree forests up to the thick tea-shrub territory of the high mountain villages of Thekaddy and Munnar, whose nature reserves hide tigers and herds of elephant.

Planning your trip

Best time to visit Kerala

By far the most comfortable time to visit Kerala is from October to March, when the weather is dry and relatively cool. April and May are intensely hot, especially on the coastal plains, with humidity building up as the monsoon approaches. The southwest monsoon hits Kerala in early June, sweeping northward up the coast; the heaviest rain comes in July and can see large parts of the state knee-deep in water for hours or even days at a time. A second, lighter monsoon begins in September or October, travelling up the east coast. If you're travelling during the monsoon you need to be prepared for extended periods of torrential rain and disruption to travel. The post-monsoon period brings cool air and clear skies – this is the best time for mountain views – while winter temperatures can drop close to zero in the higher terrain of the Western Ghats.

Getting to Kerala

Air

India is accessible by air from virtually every continent and, thanks to excellent connections through the Gulf and Southeast Asia, it's almost as easy to fly straight into Kerala as to come via the usual international gateways of Mumbai and New Delhi.

There are international airports at Kochi, Kozhikode (still listed under its old name of Calicut by some airline booking systems) and Thiruvananthapuram (Trivandrum). Any one of these makes for a relatively stress-free entry to India. Several carriers permit 'open-jaw' travel, making it possible to fly into one airport and out of another – a great option if you want to explore the full length of Kerala without having to backtrack to your point of arrival.

The cheapest return flights to Kochi from London start from around £500, but leap to £800+ as you approach the high seasons of Christmas, New Year and Easter.

From Europe Despite the increases to Air Passenger Duty, Britain remains the cheapest place in Europe for flights to India. **British Airways**, **Virgin Atlantic**, **Jet Airways** and **Air India** all fly direct from London to Mumbai, while **British Airways** also flies direct to Chennai, Bengaluru and Hyderabad.

Air India and **Jet Airways** offer direct services to Mumbai from several airports in mainland Europe, while major European flag carriers, including **KLM** and **Lufthansa**, fly to Mumbai from their respective hub airports.

If you're heading straight to Kerala, the cheapest and most convenient flights are generally with Middle Eastern or Central Asian airlines, transiting via airports in the Gulf. Several airlines from the Middle East (including **Emirates**, **Etihad**, **Gulf Air**, **Kuwait Airways**, **Qatar Airways** and **Oman Air**) offer good fares from a wide choice of British and European airports to Kochi or Thiruvananthapuram via their hub cities. This may add a couple of hours to the journey time, but allows you to avoid the more fraught route via Mumbai, which involves long immigration queues and shuttling from the international to the domestic terminal. Consolidators in the UK can quote some competitive fares, such as *www.skyscanner.net*, *www.ebookers.com*, or **North South Travel** ① *T01245-608291, www.northsouthtravel.co.uk (profits to charity)*.

Don't miss...

1 **Ayurvedic medicine at Kovalam and Varkala**, pages 45 and 46.
2 **Backwaters**, page 49.
3 **Snake boat races at Alappuzha in August**, page 59.
4 **Dusk at Fort Kochi**, page 62.
5 **Periyar National Park**, page 78.
6 **Monsoon rafting and folk culture along the River Nila**, pages 93 and 99.
7 **Pooram festival at the end of April in Thrissur**, page 99.
8 **Theyyam dances in Kerala's northern villages**, page 109.

Numbers relate to the map on page 4.

From North America From the east coast, several airlines including **Air India**, **Jet Airways**, **Continental** and **Delta** fly direct from New York to Mumbai, from where you can pick up an internal flight to any of Tamil Nadu's main airports. **American** flies from Chicago. Discounted tickets on **British Airways**, **KLM**, **Lufthansa**, **Gulf Air** and **Kuwait Airways** are sold through agents, although they will invariably fly via their country's capital city. From the west coast, your best option is to fly to Chennai via Hong Kong, Singapore or Bangkok using one of those countries' national carriers. **Air Canada** operates between Vancouver and Delhi, which also has good internal connections to Tamil Nadu. **Air Brokers International** ① www.airbrokers.com, is competitive and reputable. **STA** ① www.statravel. co.uk, has offices in many US cities, Toronto and Ontario. Student fares are also available from **Travel Cuts** ① www.travelcuts.com, in Canada.

From Australasia Qantas, **Singapore Airlines**, **Thai Airways**, **Malaysian Airlines**, **Cathay Pacific** and **Air India** are the principal airlines connecting the continents, although none have direct flights to the south. **Singapore Airlines** offers the most flexibility, with subsidiary **Silk Air** flying to Kochi and Thiruvananthapuram. Low-cost carriers, including **Air Asia** (via Kuala Lumpur), **Scoot** and **Tiger Airways** (Singapore), offer flights to Kochi at substantial savings, though long layovers and possible missed connections make this a potentially more risky venture than flying with the mainstream airlines. **STA** and **Flight Centre** offer discounted tickets from their branches in major cities in Australia and New Zealand.

Airport information The formalities on arrival in India have been increasingly streamlined during the last few years and the facilities at the major international airports greatly improved. However, arrival can still be a slow process. Disembarkation cards, with an attached customs declaration, are handed out to passengers during the inward flight. The immigration form should be handed in at the immigration counter on arrival. The customs slip will be returned, for handing over to customs officials on leaving the baggage collection hall. You may well find that there are delays of over an hour at immigration in processing passengers who need help with filling in forms. When departing, note that you'll need to have a printout of your itinerary to get into the airport, and the security guards will only let you into the terminal within three hours of your flight. Many airports require you to scan your bags before checking in and in rare cases you may also be asked to identify your checked luggage after going through immigration and security checks.

Departure charges Several Indian airports have begun charging a Passenger Service Fee or User Development Fee to each departing passenger. This is normally included in international tickets, but some domestic airlines have been reluctant to incorporate the charge. Keep some spare cash in rupees in case you need to pay the fee on arriving at the terminal.

Transport in Kerala

Air

India has a comprehensive flight network linking the major cities of the different states. Deregulation of the airline industry has had a transformative effect on travel within India, with a host of low-budget private carriers jockeying to provide the lowest prices or highest frequency on popular routes. On any given day, booking a few days in advance, you can expect to fly between Mumbai and Kochi for around US$100 one way including taxes, while booking a month in advance can reduce the price to US$60-70.

Competition from the efficiently run private sector has, in general, improved the quality of services provided by the nationalized airlines. It also seems to herald the end of the two-tier pricing structure, meaning that ticket prices are now usually the same for foreign and Indian travellers. The airport authorities, too, have made efforts to improve handling on the ground.

Although it is comparatively expensive and delays and re-routing can be irritating, flying is an option worth considering for covering vast distances or awkward links on a route. For short distances (eg Thiruvananthapuram–Kochi), and on routes where you can sleep during an overnight journey it makes more sense to travel by train.

The best way to get an idea of the current routes, carriers and fares is to use a third-party booking website such as **www.cheapairticketsindia.com** (toll-free numbers: UK T0800-101 0928, USA T1-888 825 8680), **www.cleartrip.com**, **www.makemytrip.co.in**, or **www.yatra.com**. Booking with these is a different matter: some refuse foreign credit cards outright, while others have to be persuaded to give your card special clearance. Tickets booked on these sites are typically issued as an email ticket or an SMS text message – the simplest option if you have an Indian mobile phone, though it must be converted to a paper ticket at the relevant carrier's airport offices before you will be allowed into the terminal. **Makemytrip.com** and **Travelocity.com** both accept international credit cards.

Rail

Trains can still be the cheapest and most comfortable means of travelling long distances, saving you hotel expenses on overnight journeys. Rail travel gives access to booking station Retiring Rooms, which can be useful from time to time. Above all, it provides an ideal opportunity to meet local travellers and catch a glimpse of life on the ground.

High-speed trains There are several air-conditioned 'high-speed' **Shatabdi** (or 'Century') **Express** trains for day travel, and **Rajdhani Express** ('Capital City') for overnight journeys. These cover large sections of the network but due to high demand you need to book them well in advance (up to 90 days). Meals and drinks are usually included.

Classes **A/c First Class**, available only on main routes, is the choice of the Indian upper crust, with two- or four-berth carpeted sleeper compartments with washbasin. As with all a/c sleeper accommodation, bedding is included, and the windows are tinted to the point of being almost impossible to see through. **A/c Sleeper**, two- and three-tier configurations

Train touts

Many railway stations – and some bus stations and major tourist sites – are heavily populated with touts. Self-styled 'agents' will board trains before they enter the station and seek out tourists, often picking up their luggage and setting off with words such as "Madam!/Sir! Come with me madam/sir! You need top-class hotel …". They will even select porters to take your luggage without giving you any say.

If you have succeeded in getting off the train or even in obtaining a trolley you will find hands eager to push it for you.

For a first-time visitor such touts can be more than a nuisance. You need to keep calm and firm. Decide in advance where you want to stay. If you need a porter on trains, select one yourself and agree a price before the porter sets off with your baggage. If travelling with a companion one can stay guarding the luggage while the other finds a taxi and negotiates the price to the hotel. It sounds complicated and sometimes it feels it. The most important thing is to behave as if you know what you are doing!

(known as 2AC and 3AC), are clean and comfortable and popular with middle-class families; these are the safest carriages for women travelling alone. **A/c Executive Class**, with wide reclining seats, are available on many Shatabdi trains at double the price of the ordinary **a/c Chair Car** which are equally comfortable. **First Class (non-a/c)** is gradually being phased out, and is now restricted to a handful of routes through Tamil Nadu and Kerala, but the run-down old carriages still provide a very enjoyable combination of privacy and windows that can open. **Second Class (non-a/c)** two- and three-tier (commonly called **Sleeper**) provides exceptionally cheap and atmospheric travel, with basic padded vinyl seats and open windows that allow the sights and sounds of India (not to mention dust, insects and flecks of spittle expelled by passengers up front) to drift into the carriage. On long journeys Sleeper can be crowded and uncomfortable, and toilet facilities can be unpleasant; it is nearly always better to use the Indian-style squat loos rather than the Western-style ones as they are better maintained. At the bottom rung is **Unreserved Second Class**, with hard wooden benches. You can travel long distances for a trivial amount of money, but unreserved carriages are often ridiculously crowded, and getting off at your station may involve a battle of will and strength against the hordes trying to shove their way on.

Indrail passes These allow travel across the entire Indian railway network, but you have to spend a high proportion of your time on the train to make it worthwhile. However, the advantages of pre-arranged reservations and automatic access to Foreign Tourist Quota tickets can tip the balance in favour of the pass for some travellers.

Tourists (foreigners and Indians resident abroad) may buy these passes from the tourist sections of principal railway booking offices in foreign currency, major credit cards, traveller's cheques or rupees with encashment certificates. Fares range from US$57 to US$1060 for adults or half that for children.

Indrail passes can also conveniently be bought abroad from special agents. For people contemplating a single long journey soon after arriving in India, the half- or one-day pass with a confirmed reservation is worth the peace of mind; two- or four-day passes are also sold.

The UK agent is **SDEL** ① *103 Wembley Park Dr, Wembley, Middlesex HA9 8HG, UK, T020-8903 3411, www.indiarail.co.uk*, which makes all necessary reservations and offers excellent advice. It can also book **Air India** and **Jet Airways** internal flights.

Cost A/c First Class costs about double the rate for two-tier shown below, and non a/c Sleeper class about half. Children (aged five to 12) travel at half the adult fare. Young people (12-30 years) and senior citizens (65 years and over) are allowed a 30% discount on journeys over 500 km (just show your passport).

Period	US$ A/c 2-tier	Period	US$ A/c 2-tier
½ day	26	21 days	198
1 day	43	30 days	248
7 days	135	60 days	400
15 days	185	90 days	530

Fares for individual journeys are based on distance covered and reflect both the class and the type of train. Higher rates apply on the Mail and Express trains and the air-conditioned Shatabdi and Rajdhani expresses.

Internet services Information is available online at www.railtourismindia.com, www.indianrail.gov.in, www.erail.in and www.trainenquiry.com, where you can check timetables (which change frequently), numbers, seat availability and even the running status of your train. Internet e-tickets can be bought and printed at www.irctc.in, though it's a fiendishly frustrating system to use, and paying with a foreign credit card is fraught with difficulty. If you plan to do a lot of train travel on popular routes it might be worth the effort to get your credit card recognized by the booking system. This process changes often, so your best option is to consult the very active India transport forums at www.indiamike.com.

An alternative is to seek out a local agent who sells e-tickets, which can cost as little as Rs 10 (plus Rs 20 reservation fee, though some agents charge up to Rs 150 a ticket) and can save hours of hassle; simply present the printout to the ticket collector. However, it is tricky if you then want to cancel an e-ticket which an agent has bought for you on their account.

Tickets and reservations It is possible to reserve tickets for virtually any train on the network from one of the 1000 computerized reservation centres across India. It is always best to book as far in advance as possible (usually up to 60 days). To reserve a seat on a particular train, note down the train's name, number and departure time and fill in a reservation form while you line up at the ticket window; you can use one form for up to four passengers. At busy stations the wait can take an hour or more.

You can save a lot of time and effort by asking a travel agent to get your tickets for a fee of Rs 50-100. If the class you want is full, ask if tickets are available under any of Indian Rail's special quotas. **Foreign Tourist Quota** (FTQ) reserves a small number of tickets on popular routes for overseas travellers; you need your passport and either an exchange certificate or ATM receipt to book tickets under FTQ. The other useful special quota is **Tatkal**, which releases a last-minute pool of tickets at 1000 on the day before the train departs.

If the quota system can't help you, consider buying a 'wait list' ticket, as seats often become available close to the train's departure time; phone the station on the day of departure to check your ticket's status. If you don't have a reservation for a particular train but carry an Indrail Pass, you may get one by arriving three hours early. Be wary of touts at the station offering tickets, hotels or exchange.

Timetables It's best to consult the websites listed above for the most up-to-date timetable information. Once you're on the ground, regional timetables are available cheaply from station bookstalls; the monthly *Indian Bradshaw* is sold in principal stations, and the handy but daunting *Trains at a Glance* (Rs 40) lists popular trains likely to be used by most foreign travellers. You can pick it up in the UK from **SDEL** (see page 10).

Road

Road travel is often the only choice for reaching many of the places of outstanding interest in which India is so rich. For the uninitiated, travel by road can also be a worrying experience because of the apparent absence of conventional traffic regulations and also in the mountains, especially during the rainy season when landslides are possible. Vehicles drive on the left – in theory. Routes around the major cities are usually crowded with lorry traffic, especially at night, and the main roads are often poor and slow. There are a few motorway-style expressways, but most main roads are single track. Some district roads are quiet, and although they are not fast they can be a good way of seeing the country and village life if you have the time.

Bus Buses now reach virtually every part of India, offering a cheap, if often uncomfortable, means of visiting places off the rail network. Very few villages are now more than 2-3 km from a bus stop. Most services in Kerala are operated by the government-run **Kerala State Road Transport Corporation** (KSRTC) ① *www.keralartc.com*. These buses depart from the central bus stand in every town. Larger towns and popular tourist destinations are also served by private bus operators, whose offices cluster around the main bus stand. The latter allow advance reservations, including booking printable e-tickets online (check www.redbus.in and www.viaworld.in) and, although tickets prices are a little higher, they have fewer stops and are a bit more comfortable. In the absence of trains, buses are often the only budget option. There are also many sleeper buses (a contradiction in terms); if you must take a sleeper bus, choose a lower berth near the front of the bus. The upper berths are almost always really uncomfortable.

Bus categories Though comfortable for sightseeing trips, apart from the very best 'sleeper coaches' even **air-conditioned luxury coaches** can be very uncomfortable for really long journeys. Often the air conditioning is very cold so wrap up. Journeys over 10 hours can be extremely tiring so it is better to go by train if there is a choice. **Express buses** run over long distances (frequently overnight), these are often called 'video coaches' and can be an appalling experience unless you appreciate loud film music blasting through the night. Ear plugs and eye masks may ease the pain. They rarely average more than 45 kph. **Local buses** are often very crowded, quite bumpy, slow and usually poorly maintained. However, over short distances, they can be a very cheap, friendly and easy way of getting about. Even where signboards are not in English someone will usually give you directions. Many larger towns have **minibus** services which charge a little more than the buses and pick up and drop passengers on request. Again very crowded, and with restricted headroom, they are the fastest way of getting about many of the larger towns.

Bus travel tips Some towns have different bus stations for different destinations. Booking on major long-distance routes is now computerized. Book in advance where possible and avoid the back of the bus where it can be very bumpy. If your destination is only served by a local bus you may do better to take the Express bus and 'persuade' the driver, with a tip in advance, to stop where you want to get off. You will have to pay the full fare to the first stop beyond your destination but you will get there faster and more comfortably. When an unreserved bus pulls into a bus station, there is usually an unholy scramble for seats, whilst those arriving have to struggle to get off! In many areas there is an unwritten 'rule of reservation' using handkerchiefs or bags thrust through the windows to reserve seats. Some visitors may feel a more justified right to a seat having fought their way through the crowd, but it is generally best to do as local people do and be prepared with a handkerchief or 'sarong'. As soon as it touches the seat, it is yours! Leave it on your seat when getting off to use the toilet at bus stations.

Car A car provides a chance to travel off the beaten track, and gives unrivalled opportunities for seeing something of India's great variety of villages and small towns. Until recently, the most widely used hire car was the romantic but notoriously unreliable Hindustan Ambassador. You can still find them for hire in parts of Tamil Nadu and Kerala, but they're gradually giving way to more efficient (and boring) Tata and Toyota models with mod cons such as optional air-conditioning ... and seat belts. A handful of international agencies offer self-drive car hire (**Avis**, **Sixt**), but India's majestically anarchic traffic culture is not for the faint-hearted, and emphatically not a place for those who value such quaint concepts as lane discipline, or indeed driving on your assigned side of the road. It's much more common, and comfortable, to hire not just the car but someone to drive it for you.

Car hire If you fancy the idea of being Lady Penelope and gadding about with your own chauffeur, dream no more. Hiring a car and driver is the most comfortable and efficient way to cover short to medium distances, and although prices have increased sharply in recent years car travel in India is still a bargain by western standards. Even if you're travelling on a modest budget a day's car hire can help take the sting out of an arduous journey, allowing you to go sightseeing along the way without looking for somewhere to stash your bags.

Local drivers often know their way around an area much better than drivers from other states, so where possible it is a good idea to get a local driver who speaks the state language, in addition to being able to communicate with you. The best way to guarantee a driver who speaks good English is to book in advance with a professional travel agency, either in India or in your home country. Recommended operators with English speaking drivers include **Milesworth Travel** ⓘ *www.milesworth.com*, and **Intersight** ⓘ *www.intersighttours.com*. You can, if you choose, arrange car hire informally by asking around at taxi stands, but don't expect your driver to speak anything more than rudimentary English.

On pre-arranged overnight trips the fee you pay will normally include fuel and inter-state taxes – check before you pay – and a wage for the driver. Drivers are responsible for their expenses, including meals (and the pervasive servant-master culture in India means that most will choose to sit separately from you at meal times). Some tourist hotels provide rooms for drivers, but they often choose to sleep in the car overnight to save money. In some areas drivers also seek to increase their earnings by taking you to hotels and shops where they earn a handsome commission; these are generally hugely overpriced and poor alternatives to the hotels recommended in this book, so don't be afraid to say no and insist on your choice of accommodation. If you feel inclined, a tip at the end of the tour of Rs 100 per day is perfectly acceptable.

	Tata Indica non-a/c	Tata Indigo non-a/c	Hyundai Accent a/c	Toyota Innova
8 hrs/80 km	Rs 1200	Rs 1600	Rs 2200	Rs 2500
Extra km	Rs 8	Rs 10	Rs 15	Rs 15
Extra hour	Rs 80	Rs 100	Rs 200	Rs 180
Out of town				
Per km	Rs 8	Rs 10	Rs 15	Rs 15
Night halt	Rs 200	Rs 200	Rs 300	Rs 250

Taxi Taxi travel in India is a great bargain, and in most cities in Kerala you can take a taxi from the airport to the centre for under US$15.

Yellow-top taxis in cities and large towns are metered, although tariffs change frequently. The latest rates are typically shown on a fare conversion chart which should be read in conjunction with the meter reading. Increased night time rates apply in most cities, and there might be a small charge for luggage.

Insist on the taxi meter being flagged in your presence. If the driver refuses, the official advice is to contact the police. When a taxi doesn't have a meter, you will need to fix the fare before starting the journey; ask at your hotel desk for a rough price. As a foreigner, it is rare to get a taxi in the big cities to use the meter – if they are eager to, watch out as sometimes the meter is rigged and they have a fake rate card. Also, watch out for the David Blaine-style note shuffle: you pay with a Rs 500 note, but they have a Rs 100 note in their hand.

Most airports and many major stations have booths where you can book a prepaid taxi. For slightly more than the metered fare these allow you to sidestep overcharging and give you the security of knowing that your driver will take you to your destination by the most direct route. You might be able to join up with other travellers at the booth to share a taxi to your hotel or a central point. It's OK to give the driver a small tip at the end of the journey.

At night, always have a clear idea of where you want to go and insist on being taken there. Taxi drivers may try to convince you that the hotel you have chosen 'closed three years ago' or is 'completely full'. Say that you have a reservation.

Rickshaw Auto-rickshaws (autos) are almost universally available in towns across Kerala and are the cheapest and most convenient way of getting about. It is best to walk a short distance away from a hotel gate before picking up an auto to avoid paying an inflated rate. In addition to using them for short journeys it is often possible to hire them by the hour, or for a half or full day's sightseeing. In some areas younger drivers who speak some English and know their local area well may want to show you around. However, rickshaw drivers are often paid a commission by hotels, restaurants and gift shops so advice is not always impartial. Drivers generally refuse to use a meter, often quote a ridiculous price or may sometimes stop short of your destination. If you have real problems it can help to note down the vehicle licence number and threaten to go to the police.

Cycle-rickshaws and **horse-drawn tongas** are more common in the more rustic setting of a small town or the outskirts of a large one. You will need to fix a price by bargaining. The animal attached to a *tonga* usually looks too undernourished to have the strength to pull the driver, let alone passengers.

Where to stay in Kerala

India has an enormous range of accommodation, and you can stay safely and very cheaply by Western standards right across the country. The mainstay of the budget traveller is the ubiquitous Indian 'business hotel'. These are usually within walking distance of train and bus stations, anonymous but generally decent value, with en suite rooms of hugely variable cleanliness and a TV showing 110 channels of cricket and *Bollywood MTV*. At the top end, alongside international chains like **ITC Sheraton** (ostentatious) and **Radisson Blu** (dependable), India boasts several home-grown hotel chains, best of which are the exceptional heritage and palace hotels operated by the **Taj** group.

Meanwhile, Kerala offers abundant opportunities to stay in fine style in converted mansions and farmhouses – a great way to help preserve architectural heritage while keeping your money in the local economy. While the coastal holiday belts of southern Kerala have their share of big and bland resorts, you'll also find a huge variety of individual lodgings, from porous coconut-fibre beach shacks that don't even come with a lock, to luxurious restored forts overlooking the Arabian Sea and minimalist Zen retreats hidden in paddy fields.

In the high season (October to April, peaking at Christmas/New Year and again at Easter) bookings can be extremely heavy in popular destinations such as Kovalam and Varkala. It is generally possible to book in advance by phone, fax or email, sometimes on payment of a deposit, but double check your reservation a day or two beforehand and always try to arrive as early as possible in the day to iron out problems.

Hotels → *For hotel price codes, see box, opposite.*

Price categories The category codes used in this book are based on prices of double rooms excluding taxes. They are not star ratings and individual facilities vary considerably. Modest hotels may not have their own restaurant but will often offer 'room service', bringing in food from outside; in temple towns, restaurants may only serve vegetarian food.

Off-season rates Large reductions are made by hotels in all categories out-of-season in many resorts. Always ask if any is available. You may also request the 10-15% agent's commission to be deducted from your bill if you book direct. Clarify whether the agreed figure includes all taxes.

Taxes In general most hotel rooms rated at Rs 1200 or above are subject to a tax of 10%. Many states levy an additional luxury tax of 10-25%, and some hotels add a service charge of 10% on top of this. Taxes are not necessarily payable on meals, so it is worth settling your meals bill separately. Most hotels in the **$$** category and above accept payment by credit card. Check your final bill carefully. Visitors have complained of incorrect bills, even in the most expensive hotels. The problem particularly afflicts groups, when last-minute extras appear mysteriously on some guests' bills. Check the evening before departure, and keep all receipts.

Hotel facilities You have to be prepared for difficulties which are uncommon in the West. It is best to inspect the room and check that all equipment (air conditioning, TV, water heater, flush) works before checking in at a modest hotel. Many hotels try to wring too many years' service out of their linen, and it's quite common to find sheets that are stained, frayed or riddled with holes. Don't expect any but the most expensive or tourist-savvy hotels to fit a top sheet to the bed.

In some states **power cuts** are common, or hot water may be restricted to certain times of day. The largest hotels have their own generators but it is best to carry a good torch.

Price codes

Where to stay

$$$$	over US$150	**$$$**	US$66-150
$$	US$30-65	**$**	under US$30

For a double room in high season, excluding taxes.

Restaurants

$$$	over US$12	**$$**	US$6-12	**$**	under US$6

For a two-course meal for one person, excluding drinks and service charge.

In some regions **water supply** is rationed periodically. Keep a bucket filled to use for flushing the toilet during water cuts. Occasionally, tap water may be discoloured due to rusty tanks. During the cold weather and in hill stations, hot water will be available at certain times of the day, sometimes in buckets, but is usually very restricted in quantity. Electric water heaters may provide enough for a shower but not enough to fill a bath tub. For details on drinking water, see page 17.

Hotels close to temples can be very **noisy**, especially during festivals. Music blares from loudspeakers late at night and from very early in the morning, often making sleep impossible. Mosques call the faithful to prayers at dawn. Some find ear plugs helpful.

Some hotels offer **24-hour checkout**, meaning you can keep the room a full 24 hours from the time you arrive – a great option if you arrive in the afternoon and want to spend the morning sightseeing.

Homestays

At the upmarket end, increasing numbers of travellers are keen to stay in private homes and guesthouses, opting not to book large hotel chains that keep you at arm's length from a culture. Instead, travellers get home-cooked meals in heritage houses and learn about a country through conversation with often fascinating hosts. Kerala has been particularly enthusiastic in embracing the homestay model, although the term is increasingly abused as a marketing term by small hotels. Companies specializing in homestays include **Kerala Connections**, www.keralaconnect.co.uk, **MAHout**, www.mahoutuk.com, **Pyramid Tours**, www.pyramidtravelindia.com, and **Sundale Vacations**, www.sundale.com.

Food and drink in Kerala → *For restaurant price codes, see box, above.*

Food

You'll find just as much variety in dishes crossing South India as you would on an equivalent journey across Europe. Varying combinations of spices and unique local ingredients give each region its distinctive flavour.

Kerala's cultural and religious diversity means that vegetarian food is less dominant than in the neighbouring states of Tamil Nadu and Karnataka. The two pillars of Kerala cuisine are coconut and the indigenous *matta* rice, a distinctively nutty and nutritious variety often served with its husk.

Typical dishes you'll find throughout Kerala include *appam* (a moist, crisp-edged pancake of rice flour fermented with palm toddy or wine), *idiyappam* (steamed rice flour noodles), and *puttu* (hard cylindrical cakes of rice flour and grated coconut). All of the above are generally served at breakfast with a coconut-cream based stew of meat, fish or vegetables, and washed down with Kerala's brew of choice, milky filter coffee.

Along the Kerala coast, with its largely Syrian Christian and Muslim population, you'll find excellent fish and seafood dishes. Commonly found fish include *pearlspot* and *karimeen*, and these might be served simply fried, grilled or steamed, or in a *meen molee* (a potently spiced stew laden with coconut milk and tapioca).

Also ubiquitous throughout the state are the humble snacks that appear on menus in South Indian cafés the length and breadth of India: *masala dosa* (a crispy rice pancake folded over and stuffed with a lightly spiced potato filling), *utthapam* (a cross between a pancake and a pizza, topped with tomato and onion or slices of banana), and *idli* (soft steamed rice cakes served with a spicy stew called *sambar* and coconut chutney). Every town has a slew of places serving these staples, and for less than US$1 you can fuel yourself up for a full morning's sightseeing.

Throughout India the best value food comes in the shape of the traditional *thali* (called 'meals' in Kerala and neighbouring Tamil Nadu), a complete feast often served on a banana leaf. Several curries surround the central serving of rice. A typical lunchtime *thali* will include *sambar* (thick lentil and vegetable soup), *rasam* (a hot peppery consommé) two or three curries which can be quite hot and maybe a crisp poppadum. A variety of pickles are offered – mango and lime are two of the most popular. These can be exceptionally hot, and are designed to be taken in minute quantities alongside the main dishes. Plain *dahi* (yoghurt), or *raita*, usually acts as a bland 'cooler', and there's usually a bowl of sweet *payasam* (rice pudding) to finish off.

If you're unused to spicy food, go slow. Food is often spicier when you eat with families or at local places, and certain cuisines (notably those of Andhra Pradesh and the Chettinad region of Tamil Nadu) are notorious for going heavy on the chilli. Most restaurants are used to toning things down for foreign palates, so if you're worried about being overpowered, feel free to ask for the food to be made less spicy.

Food hygiene has improved immensely in recent years. However, you still need to take extra care, as flies abound and refrigeration in the hot weather may be inadequate and intermittent because of power cuts. It is safest to eat only freshly prepared food by ordering from the menu (especially meat and fish dishes). Be suspicious of salads and cut fruit, which may have been lying around for hours or washed in unpurified tap water – though salads served in top-end hotel restaurants and places primarily catering to foreigners (eg in Fort Kochi, Varkala and Kovalam) can offer a blissful break from heavily spiced curries.

Choosing a good restaurant can be tricky if you're new to India. Many **local eateries** sport a grimy look that can be off-putting, yet serve brilliant and safe food, while swish five-star hotel restaurants that attract large numbers of tourists can dish up buffet food that leaves you crawling to the bathroom in the middle of the night. A large crowd of locals is always a good sign that the food is freshly cooked and good. Even fly-blown *dhabas* on the roadside can be safe, as long as you stick to freshly cooked meals and avoid timebombs like deep-fried samosas left in the sun for hours.

Many city restaurants and backpacker eateries offer a choice of so-called **European options** such as toasted sandwiches, stuffed pancakes, apple pies, fruit crumbles and cheesecakes. Italian favourites (pizzas, pastas) can be very different from what you are used to. Ice creams, on the other hand, can be exceptionally good; there are excellent Indian ones as well as some international brands.

India has many delicious tropical **fruits**. Some are seasonal (eg mangoes, pineapples and jackfruit), while others (eg bananas, grapes and oranges) are available throughout the year. It is safe to eat the ones you can wash and peel.

Don't leave India without trying its superb range of indigenous **sweets**. A piece or two of milk-based *peda* or Mysore *pak* make a perfect sweet postscript to a cheap dinner.

Drink

Drinking water used to be regarded as one of India's biggest hazards. It is still true that water from the tap or a well should never be considered safe to drink since public water supplies are often polluted. Bottled water is now widely available although not all bottled water is mineral water; most are simply purified water from an urban supply. Buy from a shop or stall, check the seal carefully (some companies now add a second clear plastic seal around the bottle top) and avoid street hawkers; when disposing bottles puncture the neck which prevents misuse but allows recycling.

There is growing concern over the mountains of plastic bottles that are collecting and the waste of resources needed to produce them, so travellers are being encouraged to use alternative methods of getting safe drinking water. Many hotels and restaurants provide drinking water purified using a combination of ceramic and carbon filters, chlorine and UV irradiation. Ask for 'filter water'; if the water tastes vaguely like a swimming pool it is probably quite safe to drink, though it's best to introduce your system gradually to the new water. A portable water filter is a good idea, carrying the drinking water in a plastic bottle in an insulated carrier. Always carry enough drinking water with you when travelling. It is important to use pure water for cleaning teeth.

Tea and **coffee** are safe and widely available. Both are normally served sweet, and with milk. If you wish, say 'no sugar' (*chini nahin*), 'no milk' (*dudh nahin*) when ordering. Alternatively, ask for a pot of tea and milk and sugar to be brought separately. Even in aspiring smart cafés, espresso or cappuccino may not turn out quite as you'd expect in the West.

Bottled **soft drinks** such as Coke, Pepsi, Teem, Limca, Thums Up and Gold Spot are universally available but always check the seal when you buy from a street stall. There are also several brands of fruit juice sold in cartons, including mango, pineapple and apple – Indian brands are very sweet. Don't add ice cubes as the water source may be contaminated. Take care with fresh fruit juices or *lassis* as ice is often added.

Indians rarely drink **alcohol** with a meal. In the past wines and spirits were generally either imported and extremely expensive, or local and of poor quality. Now, the best Indian whisky, rum and brandy (IMFL or 'Indian Made Foreign Liquor') are widely accepted, as are good Champagnoise and other wines from Maharashtra. If you hanker after a bottle of imported wine, you will only find it in the top restaurants for at least Rs 800-1000.

For the urban elite, refreshing Indian beers are popular when eating out and so are widely available. 'Pubs' have sprung up in the major cities. Elsewhere, seedy, all-male drinking dens in the larger cities are best avoided for women travellers, but can make quite an experience otherwise – you will sometimes be locked into cubicles for clandestine drinking. If that sounds unsavoury then head for the better hotel bars instead; prices aren't that steep. In rural India, local rice, palm, cashew or date juice *toddy* and *arak* is deceptively potent.

Festivals in Kerala

India has a wealth of festivals with many celebrated nationwide, while others are specific to a particular state or community or even a particular temple. Many fall on different dates each year depending on the Hindu lunar calendar; there's a thorough calendar of upcoming major and minor festivals at www.drikpanchang.com. ▸▸ *Local festivals are listed in the Festivals section throughout the book.*

The Hindu calendar

Hindus follow two distinct eras: The *Vikrama Samvat* which began in 57 BC and the *Salivahan Saka* which dates from AD 78 and has been the official Indian calendar since 1957. The *Saka* new year starts on 22 March and has the same length as the Gregorian calendar. The 29½ day lunar month with its 'dark' and 'bright' halves based on the new and full moons, are named after 12 constellations, and total a 354-day year. The calendar cleverly has an extra month (*adhik maas*) every 2½ to three years, to bring it in line with the solar year of 365 days coinciding with the Gregorian calendar of the West.

Some major national and regional festivals are listed below. A few count as national holidays: **26 January**: Republic Day; **15 August**: Independence Day; **2 October**: Mahatma Gandhi's Birthday; **25 December**: Christmas Day.

Major festivals and fairs

Jan New Year's Day (**1 Jan**) is accepted officially when following the Gregorian calendar but there are regional variations which fall on different dates, often coinciding with spring/harvest time in Mar and Apr.

13-16 Jan The 4-day harvest festival of **Pongal** is celebrated with great fervour in areas with a large Tamil population. Doorsteps are decorated with *kaolam* (geometric designs in coloured powder), cattle are worshipped, and vast pots of the eponymous rice dish are cooked

Feb Vasant Panchami, the spring festival when people wear bright yellow clothes to mark the advent of the season with singing, dancing and feasting.

Feb-Mar Maha Sivaratri marks the night when Siva danced his celestial dance of destruction (*Tandava*), which is celebrated with feasting and fairs at Siva temples, but preceded by a night of devotional readings and hymn singing.

Apr Vishu is Kerala's New Year, when houses are decorated with lights and firecrackers explode in the air. Pilgrims flock to the temples of Sabarimala and Guruvayur. Kerala's **Pooram** season reaches full swing, with elephant parades, fireworks and cacophonous drumming in honour of the goddess Kali. The climax of the season is the huge **Thrissur Pooram**.

Apr/May Buddha Jayanti, the 1st full moon night in Apr/May marks the birth of the Buddha.

Jul/Aug Snake boat races take place all over the Backwaters.

15 Aug is **Independence Day**, a national secular holiday is marked by special events. **Vinayaka Chaturthi**, known elsewhere in India as **Ganesh Chaturthi**, is the day when the elephant-headed god of good omen is shown special reverence. On the last of the 5-day festival after harvest, clay images of Ganesh are taken in procession with dancers and musicians, and are immersed in the sea, river or pond.

Aug/Sep Kerala's 'national festival', **Onam**, takes place over 10 days, with great processions (the biggest takes place in Thripunithara, a suburb of Kochi), snake boat races and sumptuous feasts.

Aug/Sep Janmashtami, the birth of Krishna is celebrated at midnight at Krishna temples. **Sep/Oct** The festival of **Navaratri** has many local variations throughout India. Kerala's version is based around worship of Saraswathi, the goddess of wisdom and learning. Books are worshipped, and on the tenth day (*Dasara*), children are officially initiated into reading and writing. Parades take place in Thiruvanathapuram. **Oct/Nov** Gandhi Jayanti (**2 Oct**), Mahatma Gandhi's birthday, is remembered with prayer meetings and devotional singing.

Diwali/Deepavali (*Sanskrit ideepa* lamp), the festival of lights, is celebrated particularly in North India. Some Hindus celebrate Krishna's victory over the demon Narakasura, some Rama's return after his 14 years' exile in the forest when citizens lit his way with oil lamps. The festival falls on the dark *chaturdasi* (14th) night (the one preceding the new moon), when rows of lamps or candles are lit in remembrance, and *rangolis* are painted on the floor as a sign of welcome. Fireworks have become an integral part of the celebration which are often set off days before Diwali. Equally, Lakshmi, the Goddess of Wealth (as well as Ganesh) is worshipped by merchants and the business community who open the new financial year's account on the day. Most people wear new clothes; some play games of chance.

Dec Christmas Day (**25 Dec**) sees Indian Christians celebrate the birth of Christ in much the same way as in the West; many churches hold services/Mass at midnight. There is an air of festivity in city markets which are specially decorated and illuminated.

Over **New Year's Eve** (**31 Dec**) hotel prices peak and large supplements are added for meals and entertainment in the upper category hotels. Some churches mark the night with a Midnight Mass, while the beach resorts of Varkala and Kovalam throw wild parties. Fort Kochi celebrates with a full-blown **Portugese Carnival**, culminating at midnight with the lighting of a giant effigy of Santa.

Muslim holy days

These are fixed according to the lunar calendar. According to the Gregorian calendar, they tend to fall 11 days earlier each year, dependent on the sighting of the new moon.

Ramadan is the start of the month of fasting when all Muslims (except young children, the very elderly, the sick, pregnant women and travellers) must abstain from food and drink, from sunrise to sunset. Ramadan is most widely observed in the Malabar region of northern Kerala; during this time many restaurants remain closed until sundown.

Id ul Fitr is the 3-day festival that marks the end of Ramadan.

Id-ul-Zuha/Bakr-Id is when Muslims commemorate Ibrahim's sacrifice of his son according to God's commandment; the main time of pilgrimage to Mecca (the Hajj). It is marked by the sacrifice of a goat, feasting and alms giving.

Muharram is when the killing of the Prophet's grandson, Hussain, is commemorated by Shi'a Muslims. Decorated *tazias* (replicas of the martyr's tomb) are carried in procession by devout wailing followers who beat their chests to express their grief. Hyderabad and Lucknow are famous for their grand *tazias*. Shi'as fast for the 10 days.

Responsible travel in Kerala

As well as respecting local cultural sensitivities, travellers can take a number of simple steps to reduce, or even improve, their impact on the local environment. Environmental concern is relatively new in India. Don't be afraid to pressurize businesses by asking about their policies.

Litter Many travellers think that there is little point in disposing of rubbish properly when the tossing of water bottles, plastic cups and other non-biodegradable items out of train windows is already so widespread. Don't follow an example you feel to be wrong. You can immediately reduce your impact by refusing plastic bags and other excess packaging when shopping – use a small backpack or cloth bag instead – and if you do collect a few, keep them with you to store other rubbish until you get to a litter bin.

Plastic mineral water bottles, an inevitable corollary to poor water hygiene standards, are a major contributor to India's litter mountain. However, many hotels, including nearly all of the upmarket ones, most restaurants and bus and train stations, provide drinking water purified using a combination of ceramic and carbon filters, chlorine and UV irradiation. Ask for '*filter paani*'; if the water tastes like a swimming pool it is probably quite safe to drink, though it's best to introduce your body gradually to the new water. If purifying water yourself, bringing it to a boil at sea level will make it safe, but at altitude you have to boil it for longer to ensure that all the microbes are killed. Various sterilizing methods can be used that contain chlorine (eg Puritabs) or iodine (eg Pota Aqua) and there are a number of mechanical or chemical water filters available on the market.

Bucket baths or showers The biggest issue relating to responsible and sustainable tourism is water. The traditional Indian 'bucket bath', in which you wet, soap then rinse off using a small hand-held plastic jug dipped into a large bucket, uses on average around 15 litres of water, as compared to 30-45 for a shower. These are commonly offered, except in four- and five-star hotels.

Support responsible tourism Spending your money carefully can have a positive impact. Sleeping, eating and shopping at small, locally owned businesses directly supports communities, while specific community tourism concerns, such as those operated by **The Blue Yonder** in Kerala (see page 99), provide an economic motivation for people to stay in remote communities, protect natural areas and revive traditional cultures, rather than exploit the environment or move to the cities for work.

Transport Choose walking, cycling or public transport over fuel-guzzling cars and motorbikes.

Essentials A-Z

Accident and emergency

Contact the relevant emergency service (police T100, fire T101, ambulance T102) and your embassy (see under Directory in major cities). Make sure you obtain police/medical reports required for insurance claims.

Customs and duty free
Duty free

Tourists are allowed to bring in all personal effects 'which may reasonably be required', without charge. The official customs allowance includes 200 cigarettes or 50 cigars, 0.95 litres of alcohol, a camera and a pair of binoculars. Valuable personal effects and professional equipment including jewellery, special camera equipment and lenses, laptop computers and sound and video recorders must in theory be declared on a Tourist Baggage Re-Export Form (TBRE) in order for them to be taken out of the country; in practice it's relatively unlikely that your bags will be inspected beyond a cursory x-ray. Nevertheless, it saves considerable frustration if you know the equipment serial numbers in advance and are ready to show them on the equipment. In addition to the forms, details of imported equipment may be entered into your passport. Save time by completing the formalities while waiting for your baggage. It is essential to keep these forms for showing to the customs when leaving India, otherwise considerable delays are very likely at the time of departure.

Prohibited items

The import of dangerous drugs, live plants, gold coins, gold and silver bullion and silver coins not in current use are either banned or subject to strict regulation. It is illegal to import firearms into India without special permission. Enquire at consular offices abroad for details.

Drugs

Certain areas, such as Kovalam and Varkala, have become associated with foreigners who take drugs. These are likely to attract local and foreign drug dealers but be aware that the government takes the misuse of drugs very seriously. Anyone charged with the illegal possession of drugs risks facing a fine of Rs 100,000 and a minimum 10 years' imprisonment. Several foreigners have been imprisoned for drugs-related offences in the last decade.

Electricity

India supply is 220-240 volts AC. Some top hotels have transformers. There may be pronounced variations in the voltage, and power cuts are common. Power back-up by generator or inverter is becoming more widespread, even in humble hotels, though it may not cover a/c. Socket sizes vary so take a universal adaptor; low-quality versions are available locally. Many hotels, even in the higher categories, don't have electric razor sockets. Invest in a stabilizer for a laptop.

Embassies and consulates

For information on visas and immigration, see page 27. For a comprehensive list of embassies (but not all consulates), see http://india.gov.in/overseas/indian_missions.php. Many embassies around the world are now outsourcing the visa process which might affect how long it takes.

Health

Local populations in India are exposed to a range of health risks not encountered in the Western world. Many of the diseases are major problems for the local poor and destitute and, although the risk to travellers is more remote, they cannot be ignored. Obviously 5-star travel is going to carry less risk than backpacking on a budget.

Health care in the region is varied. There are many excellent private and government clinics/hospitals. As with all medical care, first impressions count. It's worth contacting your embassy or consulate on arrival and asking where the recommended (ie those used by diplomats) clinics are. You can also ask about locally recommended medical do's and don'ts. If you do get ill, and you have the opportunity, you should also ask your medical insurer whether they are satisfied that the medical centre/hospital you have been referred to is of a suitable standard.

Before you go

Ideally, you should see your GP or travel clinic at least 6 weeks before your departure for general advice on travel risks, malaria and vaccinations. Make sure you have travel insurance, get a dental check (especially if you are going to be away for more than a month), know your own blood group and if you suffer a long-term condition such as diabetes or epilepsy make sure someone knows or that you have a Medic Alert bracelet/necklace with this information on it. Remember that it is risky to buy medicinal tablets abroad because the doses may differ and India has a huge trade in false drugs.

Vaccinations

If you need vaccinations, see your doctor well in advance of your travel. Most courses must be completed by a minimum of 4 weeks. Travel clinics may provide rapid courses of vaccination, but are likely to be more expensive. The following vaccinations are recommended: typhoid, polio, tetanus, infectious hepatitis and diptheria. For details of malaria prevention, contact your GP or local travel clinic.

The following vaccinations may also be considered: rabies, possibly BCG (since TB is still common in the region) and in some cases meningitis and diphtheria (if you're staying in the country for a long time).

Yellow fever is not required in India but you may be asked to show a certificate if you have travelled from Africa or South America. Japanese encephalitis may be required for rural travel at certain times of the year (mainly rainy seasons). An effective oral cholera vaccine (Dukoral) is now available as 2 doses providing 3 months' protection.

Websites

British Travel Health Association (UK), www.btha.org This is the official website of an organization of travel health professionals.

Fit for Travel, www.fitfortravel.scot.nhs. uk This site from Scotland provides a quick A-Z of vaccine and travel health advice requirements for each country.

Foreign and Commonwealth Office (FCO) (UK), www.fco.gov.uk This is a key travel advice site, with useful information on the country, people, climate and lists the UK embassies/consulates. The site also promotes the concept of 'know before you go' and encourages travel insurance and appropriate travel health advice. It has links to Department of Health travel advice site.

The Health Protection Agency, www. hpa.org.uk Up-to-date malaria advice guidelines for travel around the world. It gives specific advice about the right drugs for each location. It also has useful information for those who are pregnant, suffering from epilepsy or planning to travel with children.

Medic Alert (UK), www.medicalalert.com This is the website of the foundation that produces bracelets and necklaces for those with existing medical problems. Once you have ordered your bracelet/necklace you write your key medical details on paper inside it, so that if you collapse, a medic can identify you as having epilepsy or a nut allergy, etc.

Travel Screening Services (UK), www.travelscreening.co.uk A private clinic dedicated to integrated travel health. The clinic gives vaccine, travel health advice, email and SMS text vaccine reminders and screens returned travellers for tropical diseases.

World Health Organisation,

www.who.int The WHO site has links to the *WHO Blue Book* on travel advice. This lists the diseases in different regions of the world. It describes vaccination schedules and makes clear which countries have yellow fever vaccination certificate requirements and malarial risk.

Books

International Travel and Health World Health Organisation Geneva, ISBN 92-4-15802-6-7.
Lankester, T, *The Travellers Good Health Guide*, ISBN 0-85969-827-0.
Warrell, D and Anderson, A (eds), *Expedition Medicine (The Royal Geographic Society)*, ISBN 1-86197-040-4.
Young Pelton, R, Aral, C and Dulles, W, *The World's Most Dangerous Places*, ISBN 1-566952-140-9.

Language → *See Language section on page 122 for useful words and phrases.*

The state language of Kerala is Malayalam, an offshoot of the Dravidian family of South Indian languages. As elsewhere in South India, Hindi – the official national language – is little known here, and given the notorious difficulty of learning Malayalam, English acts as the lingua franca between locals and visitors. It is widely spoken in towns and cities and even in quite remote villages it is usually not difficult to find someone who speaks at least a little English. Outside of major tourist sites, other European languages are almost completely unknown. The accent in which English is spoken is often affected strongly by the mother tongue of the speaker and there have been changes in common grammar which sometimes make it sound unusual. Many of these changes have become standard Indian English usage, as valid as any other varieties of English used around the world.

Money

Indian currency is the Indian Rupee (Re/Rs). It is **not** possible to purchase these before you arrive. If you want cash on arrival it is best to get it at the airport bank, although see if an ATM is available as airport rates are not very generous. Rupee notes are printed in denominations of Rs 1000, 500, 100, 50, 20, 10. The rupee is divided into 100 paise. Coins are minted in denominations of Rs 5, Rs 2, Rs 1 and 50 paise. **Note** Carry money in a money belt worn under clothing. Have a small amount in an easily accessible place.

Exchange rates *(Mar 2014)*

UK £1 = Rs 100, €1 = Rs 85, US$1 = Rs 60.

Credit cards

Major credit cards are increasingly acceptable in the main centres, though in smaller cities and towns it is still rare to be able to pay by credit card. Payment by credit card can sometimes be more expensive than payment by cash, whilst some credit card companies charge a premium on cash withdrawals. **Visa** and **MasterCard** have a growing number of ATMs in major cities and several banks offer withdrawal facilities for Cirrus and Maestro cardholders. It is however easy to obtain a cash advance against a credit card. Railway reservation centres in major cities take payment for train tickets by Visa card which can be very quick as the queue is short, although they cannot be used for Tourist Quota tickets.

Currency cards

If you don't want to carry lots of cash, pre-paid currency cards allow you to preload money from your bank account, fixed at the day's exchange rate. They look like a credit or debit card and are issued by specialist money changing companies, such as **Travelex** and **Caxton FX**, as well as the **Post Office**. You can top up and check your balance by phone, online and sometimes by text.

Traveller's cheques (TCs)

TCs issued by reputable companies (eg Thomas Cook, American Express) are widely accepted. They can be easily exchanged at small local travel agents and tourist internet cafés but are rarely used directly for payment. Try to avoid changing at banks, where the process can be time consuming; opt for hotels and agents instead, take large denomination cheques and change enough to last for some days.

ATMs

By far the most convenient method of accessing money, ATMs are all over India, usually attended by security guards, with most banks offering some services to holders of overseas cards. Banks whose ATMs will issue cash against Cirrus and Maestro cards, as well as Visa and MasterCard, include Bank of Baroda, Citibank, HDFC, HSBC, ICICI, IDBI, Punjab National Bank, State Bank of India (SBI), Standard Chartered and UTI. A withdrawal fee is usually charged by the issuing bank on top of the conversion charges applied by your own bank. Fraud prevention measures quite often result in travellers having their cards blocked by the bank when unexpected overseas transactions occur; advise your bank of your travel plans before leaving.

Changing money

The State Bank of India and several others in major towns are authorized to deal in foreign exchange. Some give cash against Visa/MasterCard (eg ANZ, Bank of Barodawho print a list of their participating branches, Andhra Bank). American Express cardholders can use their cards to get either cash or TCs in Mumbai and Chennai. They also have offices in Coimbatore, Goa, Hyderabad, and Thiruvananthapuram. The larger cities have licensed money changers with offices usually in the commercial sector. Changing money through unauthorized dealers is illegal. Premiums on the currency black market are very small and highly risky. Large hotels change money 24 hrs a day for guests, but banks often give a substantially better rate of exchange. It is best to exchange money on arrival at the airport bank or the Thomas Cook counter. Many international flights arrive during the night and it is generally far easier and less time consuming to change money at the airport than in the city. You should be given a foreign currency encashment certificate when you change money through a bank or authorized dealer; ask for one if it is not automatically given. It allows you to change Indian rupees back to your own currency on departure. It also enables you to use rupees to pay hotel bills or buy air tickets for which payment in foreign exchange may be required. The certificates are only valid for 3 months.

Cost of travelling

Most food, accommodation and public transport, especially rail and bus, is exceptionally cheap, although inflation is pushing prices up at a drastic rate and the cost of basic food items such as rice, lentils, tomatoes and onions have skyrocketed. There is a widening range of moderately priced but clean hotels and restaurants outside the big cities, making it possible to get a great deal for your money. Budget travellers sharing a room, taking public transport, avoiding souvenir stalls, and eating nothing but rice and dhal can get away with a budget of Rs 600-900 (about US$10-15 or £6-10) a day. This sum leaps up if you drink alcohol (still cheap by European standards at about US$2, £1 or Rs 80 for a pint), smoke foreign-brand cigarettes or want to have your own wheels (you can expect to spend between Rs 150 and Rs 300 to hire a Honda per day). Those planning to stay in fairly comfortable hotels and use taxis sightseeing should budget at US$50-80 (£30-50) a day. Then again you could always check into the **Taj** in Kumarakom for Christmas and notch up an impressive US$600 (£350) bill on your B&B alone. India can be a great place to pick and choose, save a little on basic accommodation and then treat yourself to the type of meal you could only dream of affording back home. Also, be prepared to spend a fair amount more in Fort Kochi and the Backwaters, where not only is the cost of living significantly higher but where it's worth coughing up extra for a half-decent room: penny-pinch by the beach when you'll be spending precious little time indoors anyway. A newspaper costs Rs 5 and breakfast for 2 with coffee can come to as little as Rs 50 in a South Indian 'hotel', but if you intend to eat banana pancakes or pasta by the beach in Varkala, you can expect to pay more like Rs 50-150 a plate.

Opening hours

Banks are open Mon-Fri 1030-1430, Sat 1030-1230. Top hotels sometimes have a 24-hr money changing service. **Post offices** open Mon-Fri 1000-1700, often shutting for lunch, and Sat mornings. **Government offices** Mon-Fri 0930-1700, Sat 0930-1300 (some open on alternate Sat only). **Shops** open Mon-Sat 0930-1800. Bazars keep longer hours.

Safety
Personal security

In general the threats to personal security for travellers in India are remarkably small. However, incidents of petty theft and violence directed specifically at tourists have been on the increase so care is necessary in some places, and basic common sense needs to be used with respect to looking after valuables. Follow the same precautions you would when at home. There have been incidents of sexual assault in and around the main tourist beach centres, particularly after full moon parties in South India. Avoid wandering alone outdoors late at night

in these places. During daylight hours be careful in remote places, especially when alone. If you are under threat, scream loudly. Be very cautious before accepting food or drink from casual acquaintances, as it may be drugged – though note that Indians on a long train journey will invariably try to share their snacks with you, and balance caution with the opportunity to interact.

Female travellers, especially those travelling solo, may experience 'Eve teasing', the euphemism for physical harassment – an unfortunate result of the sexual repression latent in Indian culture, combined with a young male population whose only access to sex education is via dingy cybercafés. Unaccompanied women are most vulnerable in major cities, crowded bazars, beach resorts and tourist centres where men may follow them and attempt to touch them. Festival nights are particularly bad for this, but it is always best to be accompanied at night, especially when travelling by rickshaw or taxi in towns.

The most important measure to ensure respect is to dress appropriately, in loose-fitting, non-see-through clothes, covering shoulders, arms and legs (such as a *salwaar kameez*, which can be made to fit in around 24 hrs for around Rs 400-800). Take advantage, too, of the gender segregation on public transport, to avoid hassle and to talk to local women.

The best response to staring, whether lascivious or simply curious, is to avert your eyes down and away. This is not the submissive gesture it might seem, but an effective tool to communicate that you have no interest in any further interaction. Aggressively staring back or confronting the starer can be construed as a come-on.

If you are harassed, it can be effective to make a scene. Be firm and clear if you don't wish to speak to someone, and be prepared to raise an alarm if anything unpleasant threatens.

Travel advice

It is better to seek advice from your consulate than from travel agencies. Before you travel you can contact: **British Foreign & Common-wealth Office Travel Advice Unit**, T0845-850 2829, www.fco.gov.uk. **US State Department's Bureau of Consular Affairs**, Overseas Citizens Services, Room 4800, Department of State, Washington, DC 20520-4818, USA, T202-647 1488, http://travel.state.gov. **Australian Department of Foreign Affairs Canberra**, Australia, T02-6261 3305, www.smartraveller.gov.au. Canadian official advice is on www.voyage.gc.ca.

Theft

Theft is not uncommon. It is best to keep TCs, passports and valuables with you at all times. Don't regard hotel rooms as being automatically safe; even hotel safes don't guarantee secure storage. Avoid leaving valuables near open windows even when you are in the room. Use your own padlock in a budget hotel when you go out. Pickpockets and other thieves operate in the big cities. Crowded areas are particularly high risk. Take special care of your belongings when getting on or off public transport.

If you have items stolen, they should be reported to the police as soon as possible. Keep a separate record of vital documents, including passport details and numbers of TCs. Larger hotels will be able to assist in contacting and dealing with the police. Dealings with the police can be very difficult and in the worst regions, such as Bihar, even dangerous. The paperwork involved in reporting losses can be time consuming and irritating and your own documentation (eg passport and visas) may be demanded.

In some states the police occasionally demand bribes, though you should not assume that if procedures move slowly you are automatically being expected to offer a bribe. The traffic police are tightening up on traffic offences in some places. They have the right to make on-the-spot fines for speeding and illegal parking. If you face a fine, insist on a receipt. If you have to go to a police station, try to take someone with you.

If you face really serious problems (eg in connection with a driving accident), contact your consular office as quickly as possible. You should ensure you always have your international driving licence and motorbike or car documentation with you.

Confidence tricksters are particularly common where people are on the move, notably around railway stations or places where budget tourists gather. A common plea is some sudden and desperate calamity; sometimes a letter will be produced in English to back up the claim. The demands are likely to increase sharply if sympathy is shown.

Telephone

The international code for India is +91. International Direct Dialling is widely available in privately run call booths, usually labelled on yellow boards with the letters 'PCO-STD-ISD'. You dial the call yourself, and the time and cost are displayed on a computer screen. Cheap rate (2100-0600) means long queues may form outside booths. Telephone calls from hotels are usually more expensive (check the price before calling), though some will allow local calls free of charge. Internet phone booths, usually associated with cybercafés, are the cheapest way of calling overseas.

A double ring repeated regularly means it is ringing; equal tones with equal pauses means engaged (similar to the UK). If calling a mobile, rather than ringing, you might hear music while you wait for an answer.

One disadvantage of the tremendous pace of the telecommunications revolution is the fact that millions of telephone numbers go out of date every year. Current telephone directories themselves are often out of date and some of the numbers given in this book will have been changed even as we go to press. Our best advice, if a phone number in the text does not work, is to add a '2' at the beginning. **Directory enquiries**, T197, can be helpful but works only for the local area code.

Mobile phones are for sale everywhere, as are local SIM cards that allow you to make calls within India and overseas at much lower rates than using a 'roaming' service from your normal provider at home – sometimes for as little as Rs 0.5 per min. Arguably the best service is provided by the government carrier **BSNL/MTNL** but security provisions make connecting to the service virtually impossible for foreigners. Private companies such as **Airtel**, **Vodafone**, **Reliance** and **Tata Indicom** are easier to sign up with, but the deals they offer can be befuddling and are frequently changed. To connect you'll need to complete a form, have a local address or receipt showing the address of your hotel, and present photocopies of your passport and visa plus 2 passport photos to an authorized re-seller – most phone dealers will be able to help, and can also sell top-up. **Univercell**, www.univercell.in, and **The Mobile Store**, www.themobilestore.in, are 2 widespread and efficient chains selling phones and SIM cards.

India is divided into a number of 'calling circles' or regions, and if you travel outside the region where your connection is based, eg from Delhi into Rajasthan, you will pay higher charges for making and receiving calls, and any problems that may occur – with 'unverified' documents, for example – can be much harder to resolve.

Time
India doesn't change its clocks, so from the last Sun in Oct to the last Sun in Mar the time is GMT +5½ hrs, and the rest of the year it's +4½ hrs (USA, EST +10½ and +9½ hrs; Australia, EST -5½ and -4½ hrs).

Tipping
A tip of Rs 10 to a bellboy carrying luggage in a modest hotel (Rs 20 in a higher category) would be appropriate.

In upmarket restaurants, a 10% tip is acceptable when service is not already included, while in places serving very cheap meals, round off the bill with small change. Indians don't normally tip taxi drivers but a small extra is welcomed. Porters at airports and railway stations often have a fixed rate displayed but will usually press for more. Ask fellow passengers what a fair rate is.

Tourist information
There are **Government of India** tourist offices in the state capitals, as well as state tourist offices (sometimes **Tourism Development Corporations**) in the major cities and a few important sites. They produce their own tourist literature, either free or sold at a nominal price, and some also have lists of city hotels and paying guest options. The quality of material is improving though maps are often poor. Many offer tours of the city, neighbouring sights and overnight and regional packages. Some run modest hotels and midway motels with restaurants and may also arrange car hire and guides. The staff in the regional and local offices are usually helpful.

Visas and immigration
For embassies and consulates, see page 21. Virtually all foreign nationals, including children, require a visa to enter India. Nationals of Bhutan and Nepal only require a suitable means of identification. The rules regarding visas change frequently and arrangements for application and collection also vary from town to town so it is essential to check details and costs with the relevant embassy or consulate. These remain closed on Indian national holidays. Many consulates and embassies are currently outsourcing the visa process; it's best to find out in advance how long it will take. Note that visas are valid from the date granted, not from the date of entry.

Recently the Indian government has decided to issue **visas on arrival** for residents of almost all countries (Pakistan,

Sudan, Afghanistan, Iran, Iraq, Nigeria, Sri Lanka and Somalia are the exceptions) for stays of up to 30 days. The exact time frame for the change is not yet clear, so check the latest situation online before travelling.

Applications for **visa extensions** should be made to the **Foreigners' Regional Registration Offices** in New Delhi or Kolkata, or an office of the Superintendent of Police in the District Headquarters. After 6 months, you must leave India and apply for a new visa – the Nepal office is known to be difficult.

Anyone staying in India for a period of more than 180 days (6 months) must register at a convenient Foreigners' Registration Office. They will also need to get an income tax clearance exemption certificate from the Foreign Section of the Income Tax Department in Delhi, Mumbai, Kolkata or Chennai.

Tourist For most purposes you'll require a straightforward Tourist Visa. This is typically valid for 3-6 months, though citizens of some countries may be granted a 5-year visa on request. Multiple entries permitted. Rules introduced in 2010 that required visitors leaving for Nepal or Sri Lanka to remain outside India for a minimum of 2 months have since been scrapped.

Business 3-6 months or up to 2 years with multiple entry. A letter from the company giving the nature of business is required.

5 year For those of Indian origin only, who have held Indian passports.

Student Valid up to 1 year from the date of issue. Attach a letter of acceptance from Indian institution and an AIDS test certificate. Allow up to 3 months for approval.

Visa extensions Applications should be made to the Foreigners' Regional Registration Offices at New Delhi, Mumbai, Kolkata or Chennai, or an office of the Superintendent of Police in the District Headquarters. After 6 months, you must leave India and apply for a new visa – the Nepal office is known to be difficult. Anyone staying in India for a period of more than 180 days (6 months) must register at a convenient Foreigners' Registration Office.

Weights and measures

Metric is in universal use in the cities. In remote areas local measures are sometimes used. One lakh is 100,000 and 1 crore is 10 million.

Contents

Footprint features

At a glance

⊖ **Getting around** Famous for its converted rice boat backwaters tours; take the ferry for a more local route around. Bus/car journeys in the backwaters are picturesque too. Trains from Malabar to Ernakulam and on to Thiruvananthapuram.

◐ **Time required** 2 days is enough for a backwaters cruise. Allow a couple of days for Fort Kochi and a few in Varkala. A week will make Malabar a worthwhile detour. Add 3 days for inland or ghat nature, such as the Wayanad.

☼ **Weather** Hot year round. Monsoon in Jun, Jul and Aug.

✖ **When not to go** Mar and Apr are stiflingly hot.

Kerala

Thiruvananthapuram and the far south

The state capital, a pleasant city built over gently rolling coastal land, is very much a village as soon as you step away from the crowded centre. There's none of the throb, bustle and boom-time of Ernakulam, its opposite city up north, and no one could accuse it of being cosmopolitan; you'll be pushed to find a club, or bar, or even any traffic on the roads after midnight.

It is, however, a stone's throw from here to the white sands of Kovalam, still a working fishing village, albeit one that survives under the lengthening shadow cast by unchecked tourist development. The backpackers who first populated Kovalam have left it to the package holidaymakers and luxury resorts and head instead to Varkala, a pilgrimage village and beach marked out by its sheer red rock face. Inland are the little-visited forests of Ponmudi and just over the southern border lies Kanniyakumari, the sacred toe-tip of India where three seas converge.

Arriving in Thiruvananthapuram and the far south

Getting there

The international airport is 6 km from the centre, a 15-minute drive outside rush hour, and half an hour from Kovalam. It has direct flights from Colombo, the Maldives, Kuala Lumpur, Singapore and the Middle East, as well as most major Indian cities. You can hire a prepaid taxi (Rs 150) or auto (about Rs 100) into town or wait for a local bus. At the southern end of town are the central (long-distance) bus station, with services throughout Kerala and into neighbouring Tamil Nadu, and the railway station from where trains run up and down the coast. Local buses, including those bound for Kovalam, leave from the East Fort City stand opposite the fort entrance, southwest of the station. Buses to Kovalam can drop you at Waller Junction, five minutes' walk from the Samudra Beach hotels. A further 1.5 km on they turn off for the main Kovalam Bus Stand at the Ashok Hotel gate, five minutes from most southern hotels and cafés. Lighthouse Road is steep and narrow, but autos and taxis are able to drive up it. ►► See Transport, page 46.

Getting around

Thiruvananthapuram is relatively strung out, though the centre is compact. Autos or taxis are more convenient than the packed buses but bargain hard: businesses have fast acclimatized to the price naivety that goes hand in hand with package tourism. Minimum charges start at Rs 75 for taxis, Rs 15 for autos; thereafter the rate per running kilometre for cars is Rs 4.50 (non-a/c), Rs 6.50 (a/c), rickshaws Rs 3. Drivers may be reluctant to accept the going rate. If you're heading for Kovalam, budget on around Rs 250 for a taxi and Rs 175 for an auto.

Tourist information

Tourist offices have plenty of leaflets and information sheets and are very helpful. Thiruvananthapuram's main tourist office is **Kerala Tourism** ⓘ *Park View, T0471-232 1132, www.keralatourism.org, Mon-Sat 1000-1700*, where you can book day and half-day tours around the city (Rs 110 and Rs 70 respectively). There are also offices at Thampanoor Central Bus Station, the railway station and the airport.

Thiruvananthapuram (Trivandrum) → *For listings, see pages 38-48. Phone code: 0471. Population: 744,739 of 3,234,356 in the Trivandrum District.*

According to legend, the **Sri Padmanabhaswamy Temple** ⓘ *East Fort, T0471-245 0233, open 0330-0445, 0630-0700, 0830-1000, 1030-1110, 1145-1200, 1700-1815 and 1845-1920*, was built in stages to house the statue of Vishnu reclining on the sacred serpent Ananta, which was found in the forest. It was rebuilt in 1733 by Raja Marthanda Varma, king of the erstwhile kingdom of Travancore, who dedicated the whole kingdom, including his rights and possessions, to the deity. The full significance of this gift came to light in July 2011, after Kerala's High Court ordered the Travancore royal family to hand over control of the temple and its assets to the State. Upon opening the six *kallaras* (vaults) hidden beneath the temple, a team of archaeologists discovered a hoard of gold- and jewel-encrusted idols estimated to be worth at least US$22 billion in weight alone. The find instantly propelled the temple to the head of the list of India's richest religious institutions. Meanwhile, in a twist fit for Indiana Jones, a sixth vault, guarded by an iron door emblazoned with images of cobras, remains sealed while the Supreme Court and temple astrologers wrestle over legends of a powerful curse set to be unleashed if the door is ever prised open.

Thiruvananthapuram (Trivandrum)

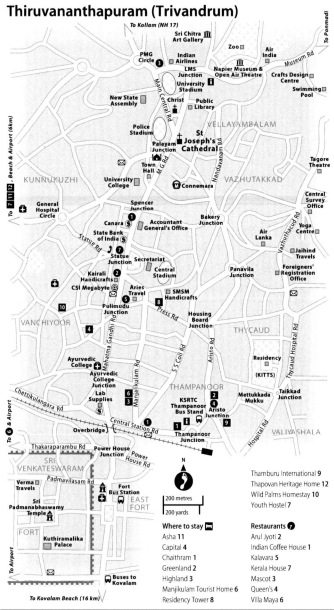

To Kollam (NH 17)
To Ponmadi

Sri Chitra Art Gallery
Zoo
Air India
Museum Rd
PMG Circle
Indian Airlines
LMS Junction
Napier Museum & Open Air Theatre
Crafts Design Centre
University Stadium
Swimming Pool
New State Assembly
Main Central Rd
Christ
Public Library
VELLAYAMBALAM
Police Stadium
St Joseph's Cathedral
Palayam Junction
Nandavanam Rd
MG Rd
Tagore Theatre
Town Hall
KUNNUKUZHI
University College
Connemara
VAZHUTAKKAD
To 7 11 12, Beach & Airport (6km)
General Hospital Circle
Spencer Junction
Bakery Junction
Central Survey Office
Canara
Accountant General's Office
Air Lanka
Yoga Centre
State Bank of India
Vazhuthacad Rd
Statue Rd
Statue Junction
Secretariat
Panavila Junction
Jaihind Travels
Foreigners' Registration Office
Kairali Handicrafts
Central Stadium
CSI Megabyte
Aries Travel
SMSM Handicrafts
Pulimudu Junction
Press Rd
Housing Board Junction
VANCHIYOOR
THYCAUD
Mahatma Gandhi Rd
Aristo Rd
S S Coil Rd
Thycaud Hospital Rd
Ayurvedic College
Residency
Ayurvedic College Junction
Lab Supplies
THAMPANOOR
(KITTS)
Chettikulangara Rd
Manjalikulam Rd
KSRTC Thampanoor Bus Stand
Aristo Junction
Mettukkada Mukku
Taikkad Junction
To 6 & Airport
Central Station Rd
Thampanoor Junction
Hospital Rd
VALIYASHALA
Overbridge
Thakaraparambu Rd
Power House Junction
Power House Rd
N
SRI VENKATESWARAM
Verma Travels
Padmavilasam Rd
Fort Bus Station
EAST FORT
200 metres
200 yards
To Airport
Sri Padmanabhaswamy Temple
FORT
Kuthiramalika Palace
Buses to Kovalam
To Kovalam Beach (16 km)

Thamburu International 9
Thapovan Heritage Home 12
Wild Palms Homestay 10
Youth Hostel 7

Where to stay
Asha 11
Capital 4
Chaithram 1
Greenland 2
Highland 3
Manjikulam Tourist Home 6
Residency Tower 8

Restaurants
Arul Jyoti 2
Indian Coffee House 1
Kalavara 5
Kerala House 7
Mascot 3
Queen's 4
Villa Maya 6

Unusually for Kerala, the temple is built in the Dravidian style associated with Tamil Nadu, with beautiful murals, sculptures and 368 carved granite pillars which support the main pavilion or *kulashekhara mandapa*. You can see the seven-storeyed *gopuram* with its sacred pool from outside; otherwise to get a closer look you first have to persuade the famously strict Kerala Brahmins to waive the Hindus-only entry restriction. It becomes easier to do so if men have donned a crisp white *dhoti*, women a sari and blouse.

The Travancore king, Maharajah Swathi Thirunal Balarama Varma, was a musician, poet and social reformer, and his palace, just next door to the temple, **Kuthiramalkia (Puthenmalika) Palace** ⓘ *Temple Rd, East Fort, T0471-247 3952, Tue-Sun 0830-1230 and 1530-1730, Rs 20, camera Rs 15*, is a fine reflection of his patronage of the arts. On the upper level a window gives an angle on scores of fine wood-carved horses that look like a huge cavalry charge, and among the portraits painted in the slightly unsettling Indian/European classical hybrid style is one from an artist who trumped his rivals by painting not just eyes that follow you around the room, but also feet. Sadly, it is ill maintained, but a gem nonetheless.

Napier Museum ⓘ *North Park Grounds, city north, T0471-231 8294, Tue-Sun 1000-1645, Wed morning only, closed public holidays*, is a spectacular landmark. The structure designed by RF Chisholm in traditional-Kerala-meets-Indo-Saracenic style, was completed in 1872. Today, it houses a famous collection of eighth to 18th-century South Indian bronzes, mostly from Chola, Vijayanagar and Nayaka periods, a few Jain and Buddhist sculptures and excellent woodcarvings. **Sri Chitra Art Gallery** ⓘ *just north of the museum, 1000-1645, closed Mon and Wed mornings, Rs 5*, has a fine catalogue of Indian art from early to modern schools: works by Raja Ravi Varma, 20th-century pioneer of the radical post-colonial school of painting, sit among paintings from Java, Bali, China and Japan, Mughal and Rajput miniatures. The Tanjore paintings are studded with semi-precious stones. The **Zoological Park** ⓘ *entrance at southwest corner of park, Tue-Sun 0900-1815, Rs 5, cameras Rs 15*, is a hilly woodland of frangipani and jacaranda with a wide collection of animals and a well-labelled botanical garden.

Kovalam and nearby resorts → *For listings, see pages 38-48. Phone code: 0471.*
Population: 25,400.

Local fishermen's boats still sit on Kovalam's narrow strip of sand right next to sunbathing tourists, but the sleepy Lakshadweep seaside village of old has now been almost completely swallowed up by package tourist infrastructure: Ayurveda parlours, trinkets, tailoring shops and tour operators line every inch of the narrow walkways behind the shore. In peak season it's something of an exotic god's waiting room, popular with pensioners, and it's safe and sedate enough for families. Backpackers tend to return off season.

North and south of Kovalam are four main stretches of beach, about 400 m long, divided by a rocky promontory on which sits the Charles Correa-designed **Leela Hotel**. The area to the north of the promontory, known as **Samudra Beach** and **Pozhikara Beach**, 5 km away offers the most sheltered bathing and the clearest water. The southern beaches, **Lighthouse Beach** and **Eve's Beach**, are more crowded and lively. Lighthouse Beach is far and away the most happening and has a long line of bars screening pirated Hollywood films, cafés selling muesli and pastries and hawkers peddling crafts or drugs; but it is still low-key compared to the costas. Further south still is where the classy resorts are clustered. **Pulinkudi Beach** and **Chowara Beach**, respectively 8 km and 10 km to the south, is where to go for hand-and-foot attentiveness, isolation, heritage-style villas and Ayurveda in luxurious surrounds.

Kovalam

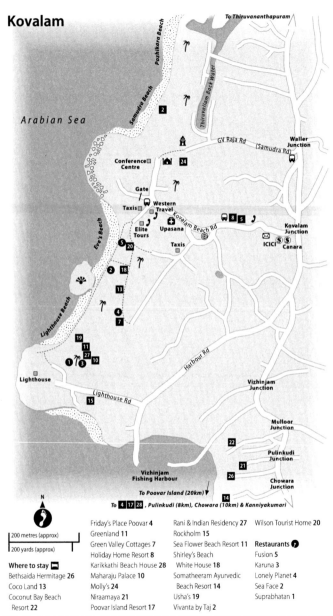

Arabian Sea

To Thiruvananthapuram

Pozhikara Beach

Samudra Beach

2

Thiruvallam Back Water

GV Raja Rd

Waller Junction

(Samudra Rd)

Conference Centre

24

Ew's Beach

Gate

Taxis

Western Travel

Kovalam Beach Rd

8 **5**

Elite Tours

Upasana

Kovalam Junction

5 **20**

Taxis

ICICI Canara

Lighthouse Beach

2 **18**

13

4

7

19

11

27 **10**

1 **3**

Lighthouse

Harbour Rd

Vizhinjam Junction

Lighthouse Rd

15

Mulloor Junction

22

Pulinkudi Junction

21

26

Chowara Junction

Vizhinjam Fishing Harbour

To Poovar Island (20km)

14

To **4** **17** **28**, Pulinkudi (8km), Chowara (10km) & Kanniyakumari

N

200 metres (approx)

200 yards (approx)

Where to stay 🛏

Bethsaida Hermitage **26**
Coco Land **13**
Coconut Bay Beach
  Resort **22**

Friday's Place Poovar **4**
Greenland **11**
Green Valley Cottages **7**
Holiday Home Resort **8**
Karikkathi Beach House **28**
Maharaju Palace **10**
Molly's **24**
Niraamaya **21**
Poovar Island Resort **17**

Rani & Indian Residency **27**
Rockholm **15**
Sea Flower Beach Resort **11**
Shirley's Beach
White House **18**
Somatheeram Ayurvedic
  Beach Resort **14**
Usha's **19**
Vivanta by Taj **2**

Wilson Tourist Home **20**

Restaurants 🍴

Fusion **5**
Karuna **3**
Lonely Planet **4**
Sea Face **2**
Suprabhatan **1**

Chowara Beach has security staff but some sunbathers still feel plagued by hawkers. **Poovar Island**, 20 km south, is accessible only by boat (Rs 200). There are now lifeguard patrols but you still need to be careful when swimming. The sea can get rough, particularly between April and October with swells of up to 6 m. From May the sea level rises, removing the beach completely in places, and swimming becomes very dangerous.

Within easy walking distance of Kovalam, sandwiched in between Lighthouse and Poovar beaches but scarcely visited by tourists, is **Vizhinjam**, a scruffy town with a low-rise string of bangle shops, banana stalls, beauticians and seamstresses sewing jasmine buds onto strings for garlands. It's hard to believe it today but Vizhinjam was once the capital of the Ay rulers who dominated South Travancore in the ninth century AD. In the seventh century they had faced constant pressure from the Pandiyans who kept the Ay chieftains under firm control for long periods. There are rock-cut sculptures in the 18th-century cave temple here, including a rough sculpture of Vinandhara Dakshinamurthi in the shrine and unfinished reliefs of Siva and Parvati on the outer wall. Today Vizhinjam is the centre of the fishing industry and is being developed as a major container port. The traditional boats are rapidly being modernized and the catch is sold all over India, but you can still see the keen interest in the sale of fish, and women taking headloads off to local markets.

Around Kovalam

South of Kovalam in Tamil Nadu is **Padmanabhapuram** ⓘ *Tue-Sun 0900-1300, 1400-1630 (last tickets 1600), Rs 200, child Rs 50 (accredited guide included, but 'donation' expected after the tour), camera Rs 25, video Rs 1500; best at 0900 before coach parties arrive*, the old wooden palace of the Rajas of Travancore. Enclosed within a cyclopean stone wall, the palace served as the capital of Travancore from 1490-1790, and is a beautiful example of the Kerala school of architecture, with fine murals, floral carvings and black granite floors. It makes a great day trip, or a neat stopover if you're heading across the Tamil Nadu border to Kanniyakumari.

At the foot of the Western Ghats, 30 km east of Thiruvananthapuram, the **Neyyar Wildlife Sanctuary** ⓘ *free, speedboat for 2 people Rs 100/150, larger boats to view the forests enclosing the lake Rs 20 per person, minibus safari Rs 10*, occupies a beautiful wooded and hilly landscape, dominated by the peak of Agasthya Malai (1868 m). The vegetation ranges from grassland to tropical, wet evergreen. Wildlife includes gaur, sloth bear, Nilgiri tahr, jungle cat, sambar deer, elephants and Nilgiri langur; the most commonly seen animals are lion-tailed macaques and other monkeys. Tigers and leopards have also been reported. **Neyyar Dam** supports a large population of crocodiles and otters; a crocodile farm was set up in 1977 near the administrative complex.

Immediately to the northeast of the Neyyar Wildlife Sanctuary a section of dense forest, **Agasthya Vanam**, was set aside as a biological park in 1992 to recreate biodiversity on a wide scale. Nearby, the **Sivananda Yoga Vedanta Dhanwantari Ashram** ⓘ *T0471-2273093, www.sivananda.org/neyyardam, minimum stay 3 days*, runs highly regarded meditation and yoga courses. It is quite an intensive schedule, with classes that start just after dawn and a strict timetable including karma yoga (meditation or devotion to God through physical labour). It is only really suitable for the hardy; others may find it heavy on Hinduism and Indian diet.

Further north sits **Ponmudi** ⓘ *buses from Trivandrum, Thampanoor Bus Stand 0530-1630; return 0615-1905, 2½ hrs,* the nearest hill station to Thiruvananthapuram, 65 km away. In a spectacular and peaceful setting, the tourist complex, though basic, serves as a good base for trekking, birdwatching and visiting the nearby minimalist deer park.

Varkala → *For listings, see pages 38-48. Phone code: 0472. Population: 42,300.*

Like Gokarna in Karnataka, Varkala is a pilgrimage centre for both backpackers and Hindus. The former come for the ruddy beach which lies at the bottom of the dramatic drop of a laterite cliff, the latter for the Vaishnavite **Janardhanaswamy Temple** and the Sivagiri Mutt of social reformer Sree Narayana Guru. The sea is far from calm (it has lifeguards for good reason), and the main beach, **Papanasam**, accessed by steep steps hacked in the cliffs, is shared between holidaymakers and fishermen. Along the cliff path, particularly along the **North Cliff**, is the tourist village high street; sizeable concrete hotels, travel agents, internet cafés, tailors stitching out endless pairs of fisherman's trousers and a huge preponderance of Kashmiri and Tibetan salespeople pushing their customary turquoise, silverware and carpets. Further north, the tourist shacks bleed into fishing village life around the **Alimood**

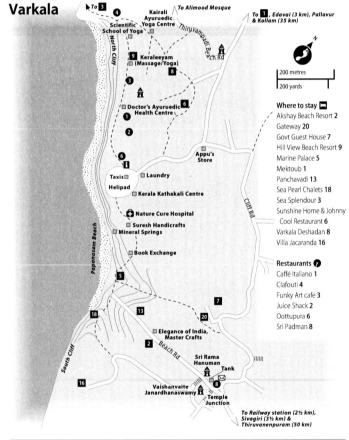

Varkala

To 3
4
Kairali Ayuruedic Yoga Centre
To Alimood Mosque
To 1, Edavai (3 km), Pallavur & Kollam (35 km)
Scientific School of Yoga
Thiruvanadi Beach Rd
9 Keraleeyam (Massage/Yoga)
8
North Cliff
3
Doctor's Ayuruedic Health Centre
1
6
2
Appu's Store
6
Taxis Laundry
Helipad
Kerala Kathakali Centre
Nature Cure Hospital
Suresh Handicrafts
Mineral Springs
Book Exchange
Papanasam Beach
Cliff Rd
5
Clafouti 4
18
13
7
20
Elegance of India, Master Crafts
2
South Cliff
Beach Rd
Sri Rama Hanuman
Tank
8
16
Vaishanvaite Janardhanaswamy
Temple Junction
To Railway station (2½ km), Sivagiri (3½ km) & Thiruvanenpuram (50 km)

200 metres
200 yards

Where to stay
Akshay Beach Resort 2
Gateway 20
Govt Guest House 7
Hill View Beach Resort 9
Marine Palace 5
Mektoub 1
Panchavadi 13
Sea Pearl Chalets 18
Sea Splendour 3
Sunshine Home & Johnny Cool Restaurant 6
Varkala Deshadan 8
Villa Jacaranda 16

Restaurants
Caffé Italiano 1
Clafouti 4
Funky Art cafe 3
Juice Shack 2
Oottupura 6
Sri Padman 8

Mosque (dress modestly). Watch your step around the cliff, particularly at night; carry a torch after dark.

The south, bordered by a golden beach, has a lovely village feel, with traditional houses built around the 13th-century temple dedicated to Vishnu. The **Arratu festival** in March-April draws thousands of visitors.

Opposite is the **Sri Rama Hanuman Temple**, whose large temple tank three wheeler drivers splash through in the morning, while women thwack their *lungis* clean on its steps. The main 'town' area (including the train station) is a further 2 km inland from Temple Junction.

A two-hour excursion takes you to **Golden Island** for a glimpse of local backwaters; there's a small temple here but it's the type of visit you'd make for the atmosphere more than anything else. A boat round the island should cost Rs 50 for the hour.

Lullaby@Varkala, www.lullabyatvarkala.in, runs tours to introduce tourists to *angan-wadis*, childcare centres for underprivileged families. The project helps feed, clothe and educate its beneficiaries.

For hotel and restaurant price codes and other relevant information, see pages 14-17.

🛏 Where to stay

Thiruvananthapuram *p31, map p32*
$$$$-$$$ Thapovan Heritage Home, Nellikunnu, T0471-248 0453, www. thapovan.com. 18 km south of town with rooms in beautiful gardens or overlooking Nellikunu beach. Ayurvedic treatments, yoga, restaurant.
$$$ Keys Hotel, Housing Board Junction (opposite the Fire Brigade), T0471-394 4100, www.keyshotels.com. Ultra-modern hotel with high-speed Wi-Fi, gym and all mod cons. Also has a women's-only floor with extra security measures.
$$$-$$ Residency Tower, Press Rd, T0471-233 1661, www.residencytower.com. Top-quality a/c rooms in a business hotel, with full facilities. Highly efficient, good restaurants, bar, rooftop pool (non-residents Rs 350). A bit swish.
$$ The Capital, off MG Rd, near the GPO, Pulimudu, T0471-247 1987, www. thecapital.in. Renovated business hotel, with smallish but clean rooms and some large, excellent value suites. Excellent rooftop restaurant. Friendly.
$$ Chaithram (KTDC), Station Rd, T0471-233 0977, www.ktdc.com. Very clean decent-sized rooms, some a/c. Next to railway and bus stand so can be noisy. Restaurant, bar.
$$ Wild Palms Homestay, Mathrubhoomi Rd, Vanchiyoor, 10 mins' walk from Statue Junction or ask for pick-up, T0471-247 1175, wildpalm@md3.vsnl.net.in. Modern welcoming guesthouse set in pretty tropical garden in the leafy suburbs. Spacious rooms, some a/c. Price includes breakfast.
$$-$ Highland, Manjalikulam Rd, T0471-233 3416, www.highland-hotels.com. Busy hotel with wide variety of clean rooms. Budget rooms good value.

$$-$ Thamburu International, Aristo Junction, T0471-232 1974 www.thamburu. com. Quiet, well-run hotel with wood-panelled walls and cheesy music in foyer. Rooms (all with TV) tend to be on small side. Some a/c rooms have balcony.
$ Asha, 200 m from airport, T0471-250 1050. Very handy for early departures. Decent rooms with bath.
$ Greenland, Aristo Junction, T0471-232 3485. Great-value rooms in quiet, immaculate, freshly renovated hotel, perfectly located within a couple of mins of both bus and railway stations. Best budget choice in town.
$ Manjalikulam Tourist Home, Manjalikulam Rd, T0471-233 0776, www. manjalikulam.com. Quiet yet central hotel with large, spotlessly clean rooms. Very friendly staff. Good value, recommended.
$ Youth Hostel (YHAI), Veli (10 km from centre), T0471-250 1230. Rooms and a dorm surrounded by coconut groves, with a pretty lagoon and clean beach. Very cheap vegetarian lunches, boating, watersports, good views.

Kovalam and nearby resorts *p33, map p34*
Long power cuts are common here, so a/c often doesn't work. Look for rooms with windows on 2 walls to get a good through-breeze. There are numerous budget cottages and rooms to let with a range of rooms from Rs 150-1000. The alleys behind **Lighthouse Beach** tend to have the cheapest accommodation. Scouts greet arrivals at the bus stand but you may pay considerably more if you use their services. You will find rooms to let, behind bars and restaurants, by walking from the Sea Rock hotel towards the lighthouse, and on the **Samudra Beach** and **GV Raja Rd** (Samudra Rd). Be aware that management of the cheaper hotels often changes hands and hotel names can change from year to year.

Rates shown here are for the high season. Prices skyrocket in all hotels for the 3-week peak period (23 Dec-7 Jan), though it still pays to bargain. High season is 1-19 Dec, 11 Jan-28 Feb; in the low season, especially May-Jul, expect 40-75% discounts.

$$$$ Friday's Place Poovar, Poover Island, T(0)9744-161636, www.fridaysplacekerala. com. Remote, watery eco-hideaway with 3 solar-powered teak and mahogany cottages and a spectacular Ark-like 'Tsunami House', set on an isolated sandbank amid rows of palms and hibiscus, frangipani and bougainvillea, run by British couple Mark and Sujeewa, the latter a Sivananda yoga teacher and reiki healer. Food is fresh, with fruit for breakfast, *thali* lunches, fish and chicken suppers. Kayaking and temple tours.

$$$$ Karikkathi Beach House, near Nagar Bhagavathy Temple at Mulloor Thottam, Pulinkudi, T0471-240 0956, www.karikkathi beachhouse.com. 2 doubles with linked lounge, palm thatch roof, no a/c or TV, perfect for honeymooners or those used to being kept; the house comes with private beach, chef, waiter and servants. There's a cottage should families or groups need extra beds.

$$$$ Niraamaya, Pulinkudi, near Kovalam, T0471-226 7333, www.niraamaya.in. Sitting high on a rocky bluff between Kovalam and Kannyukamari, this elite resort boasts a world-class spa and offers Ayurveda treatments from its beautifully designed complex. There are just 21 traditional Keralite cottages, with 4-posters, big plantation chairs and open-air bathrooms, spread over 9 ha of jackfruit, bamboo, cinnamon, mango, frangipani, palm and hibiscus trees. Excellent Sivananda yoga on a one-on-one basis at an open-air pavilion overlooking the sea.

$$$$ Poovar Island Resort, Poovar Island, T0471-221 2068, www.poovarislandresort. com. Award-winning boutique hotel with 'floating' cottages where the backwaters meet the sea. facilities include pool, handicrafts, Ayurveda, watersports.

$$$$ Vivanta by Taj, GV Raja Vattapara Rd, Kovalam, T0471-661 3000, www. vivantabytaj.com. Appealing and luxurious Balinese-flavoured complex set in 4 ha of tropical grounds with superb views of the sea, infinity pool, excellent spa, gym and Wi-Fi.

$$$$-$$$ Bethsaida Hermitage, Pulinkudi, T0471-226 7554, www. bethsaidahermitage.com. Eco-friendly stone and bamboo beach *cabanas* surrounded by coconut groves. Profits support a variety of charitable projects. Family-friendly, informal and unpretentious.

$$$$-$$$ Coconut Bay Beach Resort, Mulloor, T0471-2480 566, www.coconutbay. com. Spacious stone villas on beach, good restaurant, friendly. Secluded location in traditional fishing village. Recommended.

$$$$-$$$ Somatheeram Ayurvedic Beach Resort, Chowara Beach, south of Kovalam, T0471-226 8101, www. somatheeram.in. Kerala's 1st Ayurvedic resort and also the repeat winner of the state's competition to find the best. Its cottages and traditional Keralite houses set in coconut groves are dotted over a steep hill above the beach. If you want more peace, and the use of an oyster-shaped pool with whirlpool, stay at sister resort, **Manaltheeram**. 15 doctors and 90 therapists work in 48 treatment rooms at the shared Ayurvedic facilities. British-based holistic health and beauty therapist, **Bharti Vyas**, T+44(0)20-7935 5312 (UK), www.bharti-vyas.com, leads 10-day retreats here, or join a yoga retreat with uplifting American vinyasa flow teacher, **Shiva Rea**, www.yogaadventures.com.

$$$ Molly's, Samudra Beach Rd, Kovalam, T0471-326 2099, www.mollyskovalam.com. 2-storey hotel set around a pool. Each room has a terrace overlooking a jungly thicket of coconuts. The restaurant, which serves Mexican, European, Indian and tandoor food, is very popular.

$$$-$$ Maharaju Palace, Lighthouse Beach, T(0)9946-854270, www.maharajupalace.nl. Beautiful, shady garden setting, quiet and set back from beach. 6 very clean rooms inside and outside cottages complete with chandeliers and frou-frou interiors. Genial staff, very popular.

$$$-$ Holiday Home Resort, Beach Rd, T0471-248 0497, www.holidayhomeresort. net. Cute cottages amid a tree-filled, shady garden with hammocks to laze in. Serene location 10 mins' walk from beach. Excellent, friendly service from the helpful manager, Shar. Camping, with own tent, is possible (Rs 150).

$$ Kailasam Yoga and Ayurveda Holidays, Kovalam, T0471-248 4018, book through **Free Spirit Travel**, T+44 (0)127-356 4230 (UK), www.yogaindia.co.uk. Peaceful oasis set up by a yoga teacher and Ayurvedic physician. Yoga classes held in tiled areas under coconut-leaf roofs, surrounded by trees and open-sided to catch the sea breezes. Price includes all yoga classes.

$$ Rockholm, Lighthouse Rd, T0471-248 0406, www.rockholm.com. Very pleasant hotel owned by an Anglo-Indian family with cheerful staff. Good-sized rooms, with balcony, in a wonderful position just above the lighthouse. Direct access to beach. Good terrace restaurant.

$$-$ Coco Land, between Lighthouse Beach and Eve's Beach, T0471-653 3591, cocoheritage@yahoo.com. Bamboo huts and 'luxury' wood cottages in a little garden set back from the beach. Cottages boast TVs, a/c and hot water. Friendly management. Recommended.

$$-$ Hotel Greenland, Lighthouse Beach, T0471-248 6442, hotelgreenland@yahoo. com. Friendly female manger has a variety of spotlessly clean rooms set amongst her flowery garden. All have porch, fly-screens, 4 have kitchenettes and TV. Cheaper rooms are excellent value. Recommended.

$$-$ Sea Flower Beach Resort, Lighthouse Rd, T0471-248 0554, www. seaflowerkovalam.com. Great location

right on the shore. Good-sized rooms with decent bath and balcony. Helpful staff, good value, big discounts for long stays.

$ Green Valley Cottages, between Lighthouse Beach and Eve's Beach, T0471-248 0636, indira_ravi@hotmail.com. Spick and span simple rooms with fly-screens and sit-outs. Good value.

$ Hotel Rani, Lighthouse Beach, T(0)9995-566039, www.hotelrani.com. Basic, well-maintained rooms that open out onto a communal veranda. Friendly owner.

$ Shirley's Beach White House, between Lighthouse Beach and Eve's Beach, T(0)9447-224902, www.shirleysbeach.com. The sea-facing rooms here are a cut above other hotels in this price range. All are breezy and painted a cheerful blue, some with balcony. The owner is a wealth of knowledge. Quiet location, very good value. Recommended.

$ Usha's, Lighthouse Beach, T0471-279 0563. Good little cheapie in the winding alleys behind the beach. Basic rooms, all with bath and fly-screens. Run by the genial Usha and her family.

$ Wilson Tourist Home, up path behind Neelkantha, T0471-248 0052. Clean, quiet rooms with bath, balcony, fan, some with a/c. Open-air restaurant, pretty garden, helpful service. Recommended.

Around Kovalam p35

$$$$ Duke's Forest Lodge, Anappara, near Ponmudi, T0471-226 8822, www. dukesforest.com. 5 luxury villas, each with its own plunge pool, set on organic estate. Great trekking.

$ Government Guest House, Ponmudi, T0471-289 0211. 24 rooms and 10 cottages, in attractive gardens surrounded by wooded hills, spartan facilities but spacious rooms, restaurant serves limited but reasonable vegetarian meals, beer available, also a post office and general store.

Varkala *p36, map p36*

There are at least 50 guesthouses, plus rooms in private houses. The **North Cliff** area is compact, so look around until you find what you want: the northernmost area is where the most laid-back, budget options are and has the most character, while the far south side has a few fancier places. None, however, is actually on the beach. Outside the high season of Nov-Mar, prices drop by up to 50%. During the monsoon (Jun-Jul) many close.

$$$ Varkala Deshadan, Kurakkanni Cliff, T0470-320 4242, www.deshadan.com. Scrupulously clean Chettinadu-style a/c bungalows set around a large pool. Price includes breakfast.

$$$ Villa Jacaranda, Temple Rd West, South Cliff, T0470-261 0296, www.villa-jacaranda. biz. A delightful guesthouse, home with 5 huge rooms elegantly but sparely decorated. Jasmine, birds of paradise and magnolia blossoms are tucked into alcoves, there's a lotus-filled pond and tropical garden and everything is immaculately maintained. Guests have their own keys and entrance. Really special.

$$$-$ Marine Palace, Papanasam Beach, T0471-260 3204, www.varkalamarine.com. 12 rooms in total with 3 lovely old-style wooden rooms with balconies and a sea view. The honeymoon suite has a truly gigantic bed. Good service and nice tandoori restaurant on the beach. Recommended.

$$ Mektoub, Odayam Beach, T(0)9447-971239. Beautiful rustic-mystic hideaway – a place of candles and incense smoke. Charming owner, utterly peaceful, and a minute from uncrowded sand.

$$-$ Akshay Beach Resort, Beach Rd (about 200 m from beach), T0470-260 2668. Wide variety of bright, clean rooms. Quiet location away from the cliff. Restaurant, TV lounge, good value.

$$-$ Hill View Beach Resort, North Cliff, T0470-260 5744, www.varkalahillview. neehaarika.org. Self-contained cottages and budget rooms in a smart resort. Internet, airport pick-up, hot water.

$$-$ Sea Pearl Chalets, Beach Rd, T0470-260 0105, www.seapearlchalets. com. Circular thatched huts perched scarily near the cliff edge. Great views, breakfast included. Recommended.

$ Government Guest House, towards **The Gateway** (see Restaurants), T0470-260 2227. Immense, high-ceilinged rooms with marble floors and big baths, in the leafy former summer residence of the maharaja. Isolated, idyllic and quiet. Book in advance, recommended.

$ Panchavadi, Beach Rd, T0470-260 0200, www.panchavadi.com. Excellent location close to beach. Very clean and secure with simple rooms. Budget rooms very good value. Restaurant, helpful staff. Recommended.

$ Sea Splendour, North Cliff end, Odayam Beach, T0470-266 2120, www.seasplendour. com. Homely choice with simple rooms in retired teacher's guesthouse. Excellent home cooking (unlimited and spoilt for choice), very peaceful.

$ Sunshine Home/Johnny Cool & Soulfood Café, North Cliff, Varkala Beach, T(0)9341-201295. Colourful, chilled-out Rasta house set back off the cliff. Bongo drums and Marley posters abound. There's a variety of rooms, some with balcony, plus a little standalone thatched cottage out the back. The café does pastas, noodles, fish and chips – but in its own sweet time.

❷ Restaurants

Thiruvananthapuram *p31, map p32*

$$$ Villa Maya, Airport Rd, Subash Nagar, Enchakkal Westfort Rd, T0471-257 8901. One of the most beautiful restaurants in this book, set in a restored 18th-century Dutch villa surrounded by fountains. Dishes span a broad range of cuisines, from traditional Kerala curries to Israeli or Moroccan specials. It's pricey and they don't serve alcohol, but this is a superb choice for a splurge.

$$ Kalavara, Kalavara Hotel, Press Rd, T0471-232 2195. Indian, Continental,

Chinese, fast food (burgers, shakes), takeaway. Food average, slow service but good-value buffets in upstairs thatched section with a patch of garden. Good ambience, limited views.

$$ Kerala House, near Statue Junction, T0471-247 6144. Keralite cuisine in the basement of shopping complex. Slow for breakfast but newspapers available, outside seating in the evening in roadside car park area is cheaper. Colourful and fun place to pass some time, even if the food arrives cold. Try *neem*, *kappa* and rice (delicious fish with tapioca), or inexpensive chicken dishes with coconut; bakery in the complex does excellent samosas and puffs.

$$ Mascot, Mascot Hotel, Museum Rd. Excellent lunchtime buffet, pleasant, 24-hr coffee shop for all types of snacks, good value, a cool haven at midday.

$$ Queen's, Aristo Junction. Indian non-vegetarian. Chilli chicken recommended.

$ Arul Jyoti, MG Rd, opposite Secretariat. South Indian vegetarian. With a/c family room, clean, wide choice of good-value dishes, try jumbo *dosas*. Great Tamil Nadu *thalis*.

$ Indian Coffee House, 2 on MG Rd, with others near YWCA, north of the Secretariat, and near KSRTC Bus Stand (the latter designed by the English architect Laurie Baker). Worth seeing, excellent value coffee and snacks.

Kovalam and nearby resorts *p33, map p34*

There are hundreds of restaurants here. Service can be slow, and quality hit-and-miss since management often changes hands. Below is a very short list of those that have proved consistent. The restaurant at the **Taj** is good, if predictable. **The Leela** hotel Sun brunch has a giant salad counter and loud live music. Avoid 'catch of the day' on Sun – it's unlikely to be fresh. Some restaurants will screen pirated DVDs, sometimes to compensate for underwhelming cuisine.

$$ Fusion, Eve's Beach, T0471-248 4153. Kovalam's take on fusion food doesn't really pull it off but the cold coffees are exceptional and the menu has a nice varied mix of international and Indian food.

$$ Rockholm Hotel, (see Where to stay), Lighthouse Rd. Very good international food and tandooris served on a pleasant terrace with beautiful views, especially early morning.

$$ Sea Face, Eve's Beach. Breezy raised terrace on the beach by a pleasant pool. Varied choice including versatile fish and seafood. Friendly and attentive.

$ Karuna, Lighthouse Beach. Excellent Keralite breakfasts, home-made brown bread, decent coffee.

$ Lonely Planet, between Lighthouse Beach and Eve's Beach. Wholesome, mildly spiced Ayurvedic vegetarian food. Set around a pond with ducks – and mosquitoes. Sells recipe books and runs cookery courses.

$ Suprabhatan, Lighthouse Beach, opposite **Hotel Greenland**. South and North Indian vegetarian meals.

Varkala *p36, map p36*

There are numerous restaurants along North Cliff, most with facsimile menus, slow service and questionable kitchens; take extra care with drinking water here. 'Catch of the day' splayed out for you to inspect, usually costs Rs 100-150 depending upon the type/size of fish, but make sure you don't get 'catch of yesterday' (fresh fish keep their glassy eyes and bright silvery scales). Many restaurants close out of season.

$$$ The Gateway, Gateway Hotel, near **Government Guest House**. Every Sun 1230-1530 (Rs 300, includes pool use). Good-value eat-all-you-want buffet, delicious rich vegetarian cuisine.

$$ Caffé Italiano, North Cliff, T(0)9846-053194. Good Italian and seafood, but quite pricey.

$$ Sri Padman, near Hanuman Temple, T0472-260 5422. **Sri Padman**'s terrace overlooking the temple tank offers the best non-beachfront position in town. Come here for South Indian vegetarian breakfasts served in big stainless steel *thali* trays, and oily *parathas* to sop up spicy curries and coconut chutneys.

$ Clafouti, Clafouti Hotel, North Cliff (see Where to stay). Fresh pastries and cakes, but standards seem to drop when the French-Keralite owners are away.

$ Funky Art Café, North Cliff. Eclectic multi-cuisine menu. Sometimes hosts local bands playing Varkala versions of Western rock songs, which can be an amusing diversion while waiting for the incredibly slow service.

$ The Juice Shack, cliffside Varkala, turn off at Tibetan market. Shady little spot with healthy juice, good coffee and excellent toasted sandwiches. Brilliant for breakfast – they even have Marmite.

$ Oottupura, cliffside Varkala, near helipad, T0472-260 6994. A Varkala institution. Excellent 100% vegetarian with 60 curries and everything from Chinese to macaroni cheese. Breakfast can be *iddlies* or toasted sandwiches, all served under a giant pistachio tree covered in fairy lights.

⏏ Entertainment

Thiruvananthapuram *p31, map p32*
Performances of *Kalarippayattu*, Kerala's martial art, can be seen through: **CVN Kalari**, East Fort, T0471-247 4182 (0430-0830); and **Balachandran Nair Kalari Martial Arts Gymnasium**, Parasuvaikal, T0471-223 2686, www.kalari.in.

Kovalam and nearby resorts *p33, map p34*
Kalakeli Kathakali Troupe, T0471-248 1818. Daily at hotels including **Ashok** and **Neptune**, Rs 100.

Varkala *p36, map p36*
Varkala is a good place to hang out, chill and do yoga but there's no organized

nightlife to speak of, only impromptu campfire parties.

Kerala Kathakali Centre, by the helipad, holds a daily *Kathakali* demonstration (Rs 150, make-up 1700-1800, performance 1830-2000). The participants are generally students of the art rather than masters.

❂ Festivals

Thiruvananthapuram *p31, map p32*
In 2010 the city hosted an outlier of the **Hay Festival**, featuring authors including Vikram Seth and William Dalrymple and gigs by the likes of Bob Geldof. It's hoped it will become an annual event. Check out www.hayfestival.com/kerala.

Mar Chandanakuda, at Beemapalli, a shrine on Beach Rd 5 km southwest of the railway station. 10-day festival when local Muslims go to the mosque, holding incense sticks and pots. Marked by sword play, singing, dancing, elephant procession and fireworks.

Mar-Apr (Meenam) and Oct-Nov (Thulam) **Arattu** is the closing festival of the 10-day celebrations of the Padmanabhaswamy Temple, in which the deity is paraded around the temple inside the fort and then down to the sea.

Sep/Oct Navaratri at the special *mandapa* in Padmanabhaswamy Temple. Several concerts are held which draw famous musicians. **Thiruvonam week** in Sep.

1-10 Oct Soorya Dance Festival.
Nov-Mar A similar **Nishangandhi Dance Festival** is held at weekends when all-important classical Indian dance forms are performed by leading artistes at Nishagandhi open-air auditorium, Kanakakkunnu Palace.

⬭ Shopping

If shopping, bear in mind that prices are relatively high here: traders seldom honour the standard rates for 92.5 silver, charging by piece not weight.

Thiruvananthapuram *p31, map p32*
Shopping areas include the **Chalai Bazar**, the **Connemara Market** and the main road from Palayam to the East Fort. Usually open 0900-2000 (some take a long lunch break). Although ivory goods have now been banned, inlay on woodcarving and marquetry using other materials (bone, plastic) continue to flourish. *Kathakali* masks and traditional fabrics can be bought at a number of shops.

The shopping centre opposite East Fort Bus Stand has a large a/c shop with a good selection of silks and saris but is not cheap. *Khadi* recommended from shops on both sides of MG Rd, south of Pulimudu Junction.
Co-optex, Temple Rd. Good for fabrics and *lungis*.
Handloom House, diagonally across from Partha's. Has an excellent range of fabrics, clothes and export quality dhurries.
Partha's, towards East Fort. Recommended.
Premier Stationers, MG Rd, opposite Post Office Rd. The best best in town.
Raymonds, Karal Kada, East Fort. Good selection of men's clothing.

Handicrafts
Gift Corner and **Natesan Antique Arts**, MG Rd. High-quality goods including old dowry boxes, carved wooden panels from old temple 'cars', miniature paintings and bronzes.
Gram Sree, MG Rd. Excellent village crafts.
Kairali, MG Rd. Items of banana fibre, coconut, screw pine, mainly utilitarian, also excellent sandalwood carvings and bell-metal lamps, utensils.
Kalanjali, Palace Garden, across from the museum. Recommended.
SMSM Handicrafts Emporium, behind the Secretariat. Government-run, heaps of items reasonably priced.

Kovalam and nearby resorts *p33, map p34*
Numerous craft shops, including Kashmiri and Tibetan shops, sell a wide range of goods. Most are clustered around the bus stand at the gate of the Ashok with another group to the south around the lighthouse. Good-quality paintings, metalwork, woodwork and carpets at reasonable prices. Gems and jewellery are widely available but it is notoriously difficult to be sure of quality.

Tailoring is available at short notice and is very good value with the fabrics available. Charges vary, about Rs 50-80 per piece.
Brother Tailors, 2nd Beach Rd.
Raja, near hotel **Surya**.
Suresh, next to **Garzia** restaurant.
Zangsty Gems, Lighthouse Rd. Sells jewellery and silver and has a good reputation for helpfulness and reliability.

Varkala *p36, map p36*
Most of the handicraft shops are run by Kashmiris, who will tell you that everything (including the tie-dye T-shirts) is an antique from Ladakh.
Elegance of India and **Mushtaq**, Beach Rd. Sell Kashmiri handicrafts, carpets, jewellery, etc, reported as honest, will safely air-freight carpets and other goods.
Satori, T(0)9387-653261. Cliff-top boutique, selling pretty Western clothes made with local fabric and jewelled Rajasthani slippers.
Suresh, on path south from helipad. Handicrafts from Karnataka.

⚙ What to do

Thiruvananthapuram *p31, map p32*
Body and soul
Institute of Yogic Culture, Vazhuthacaud, T0471-304 9349, www.pillaisyogicculture. com. Yoga therapy, Ayurvedic massage.
Sivananda Ashram, Neyyar Dam, T0471-227 3093, www.sivananda.org/ndam. One of India's most highly regarded yoga teacher training programs.

Swimming
Mascot Hotel, Cantonment Rd, has a big pool. Small rooftop pool at **Residency Tower** (0700-1900, Rs 250), with great views. **Waterworks**, pool near museum, T0471-231 8990.

Tour operators

IATA-approved agencies include:

Great India Tour Co, New Corporation Bldg, Palayam, T0471-301 1500, www.gitc.travel. Offers afternoon city tours, among others. Reliable but pricey.

KTDC, **Hotel Chaithram**, Station Rd, T0471-233 0031, www.ktdc.com. Can arrange 2- to 3-day tours to Munnar and Thekkady and also runs the following local tours:

City tour: daily 0730 and 1300, 5½ hrs including Padmanabhapuram, Puthenmalika Palace, Shangumugham beach and Napier Museum, Rs 250 (Padmanabhapuram is closed on Mon).

Kanniyakumari: daily 0730-2100, including Kovalam, Padmanabhapuram and Kanniyakumari, Rs 550. Tours can feel quite rushed with little time spent at sights.

TourIndia, MG Rd, T0471-233 0437, www.tourindiakerala.com. The pioneers of backwater tourism and Periyar's Tiger Trails trekking program, highly recommended for innovative and unusual experiences, eg treehouse holidays or sport fishing off Fort Kochi.

Trekking and birdwatching

Trekking is best Dec-Apr. Obtain permission first from the Chief Conservator of Forests (Wildlife), Forest HQ, Thiruvananthapuram, T0471-232 2217, or the Assistant Wildlife Warden at Neyyar Dam, T0471-227 2182.

Kovalam and nearby resorts *p33, map p34*

Body and soul

Ayurvedic treatments are also offered by most upmarket resorts (a massage will set you back about Rs 700).

Dr Franklin's Panchakarma Institute and Research Centre, Chowara, T0471-248 0870, www.dr-franklin.com. The good doctor's family have been in Ayurveda for 4 centuries, and he himself is the former district medical officer of the Keralan government. Programmes include treatment for infertility, sluggishness, paralysis and obesity. 15-day

body purification therapy (*panchakarma* and *swetakarma*) costs US$714. 21-day *Born To Win* programme US$968. Others include *You and your spine*, *Body Mind Soul*, and there are age-reducing treatments including body immunization and longevity treatments (28 days, US$1290). The slimming programme takes 28 days, US$1200. 51-day *panchakarma*, US$2390. Cheaper treatments include: face pack US$7, 1-hr massage US$17. Also training courses in massage, Ayurveda and *panchakarma*.

Medicus, Lighthouse Rd, T0471-248 0596. Mrs Babu has a loyal clientele, many of whom return year after year.

Padma Nair, Pink Flowers, Lighthouse Beach, T(0)9895-882915, www.yogashala.in. One of *Kalaripayattu* master Balachandran Nair's students, Padma Nair has 10-day massage programmes at her village home from US$180.

Vasudeva, T0471-222 2510, in the Rohith Hotel (near Green Land). Simple but with experienced professionals.

Fishing

Can readily be arranged through the hotels, as can excursions on traditional catamarans or motor boats. You may be promised corals and beautiful fish just offshore but don't expect to see very much.

Indian martial arts

Guru Balachandran Nair, is the master of the **Indian School of Martial Arts**, Parasuvykal, 20 km from Trivandrum, T0471-272 5140, www.kalari.in. This is a college teaching *Kalaripayattu*, India's traditional martial art, as well as *Kalarichikitsa*, an ancient Indian healing tradition combining Ayurveda with *Marma* therapy, which manipulates the vital pressure points of the body to ease pain. A fighter would have had an intimate knowledge of these points to know what to harm or how to heal. A fascinating place to stay.

Tour operators

There are dozens of tour operators on the roads leading down to the beach and on the beachfront. Nearly all of them offer money exchange, onward travel booking and backwater tours.

East India Premier Tours, behind Neelkantha Hotel, between Lighthouse and Eve's Beach, T0471-248 3246. Can suggest unusual hotels.

Great Indian Travel, Lighthouse Rd, T0471-248 1110, www.keralatours.com. Wide range of tours, exchange, eco-friendly beach resorts.

Visit India, Lighthouse Rd, T0471-248 1069. Friendly and helpful, exchange, short backwater tours from Thiruvallam.

Varkala *p36, map p36*

Body and soul

Keraleeyam, North Cliff. One of the best of the many yoga/Ayurvedic massage centres.

Lakshmi Herbal Beauty Parlour, Clafouti Hotel (see Where to stay). Individual attention, amazing massages plus waxing, henna, etc.

Nature Cure Hospital, North Cliff. Opened in 1983, treats patients entirely by diet and natural cures including hydrotherapy, chromotherapy (natural sunbath with different filters) and mud therapy, each treatment normally lasting 30 mins.

Naturomission Yoga Ashram, near the helipad. Runs 1-, 2- and 7-day courses in yoga, massage, meditation, and healing techniques. Payment by donation.

Scientific School of Yoga, Naturopathy and Massage, Diana Inn, North Cliff, T0470-320 6294. 10-day yoga and massage course (2 classes daily), Rs 500, professionally run by English-speaking doctor. Also has a shop selling Ayurvedic oils, soaps, etc.

Tour operators

Most hotels offer tours, air tickets, backwater trips, houseboats, etc, as do the many agents along North Cliff.

JK Tours & Travels, Temple Junction Varkala, T0802-668 3334. Money exchange, daily 0900-2100.

🚌 Transport

Thiruvananthapuram *p31, map p32*

Air The airport, T0471-250 1426, is 6 km away from the beach. **Transport to town:** by local bus no 14, prepaid taxi (Rs 150) or auto (about Rs 100, 20 mins). Confirm international bookings and arrive in good time. Expect inflated prices at refreshments counter, though you can get cheap tea and coffee in the final lounge after security check. Banks at the airport are outside arrivals. **Johnson & Co** travel agent opposite domestic terminal, T0471-250 3555. Note that the teminal is closed at night.

Airlines Sri Lankan Airlines, Spencer Bldg, MG Rd, T0471-247 1810; **Kuwait Airways**, airport, T0471-250 1401; **Indian Airlines**, Mascot Sq, T0471-231 6870 (airport T0471-250 1537), and **Air India**, Museum Rd, Velayambalam, T0471-231 0310 (airport T0471-250 1426).

Domestic departures include: **Indian Airlines** to **Bengaluru**, **Chennai**, **Delhi** and **Mumbai**. Air India to **Mumbai**. Jet Airways to **Chennai** and **Mumbai**.

International departures include: **Air India Express** to several **Gulf** destinations; Emirates to **Dubai**; Etihad to **Abu Dhabi**. Maldivian to **Malé**; Silk Air and Tiger Airways to **Singapore**; Sri Lankan to **Colombo**.

Bus Local: City Bus Stand, T0471-246 3029. Green buses have limited stops; yellow/red buses continue through town up to museum. Blue/white bus (No 888) to **Kovalam** goes from East Fort Bus Station (30 mins, Rs 9).

Long distance: Buses leave from KSRTC Bus Station, Station Rd, near railway station, T0471-232 3886. Buses to **Kanniyakumari** via **Nagercoil** or direct, 0530, 0930, 1000,

1200, 1500, 1600 and 1830 (2½ hrs, Rs 40) and frequent departures to **Kozhikode**, (10 hrs, Rs 200) via **Kollam** (2½ hrs, Rs 44), **Alappuzha** (4 hrs, Rs 96), **Ernakulam/Kochi** (5½ hrs, Rs 129), and **Thrissur** (7 hrs, Rs 173). You can include a section of the backwaters on the way to Kochi by getting a boat from Kollam (shared taxis there cost Rs 60 each, see below). TNSTC to **Chennai, Coimbatore, Cuddalore, Erode, Kanniyakumari, Madurai** from opposite the Central Railway station.

Rickshaw Rickshaws to the Kovalam beach area should cost around Rs 70-100. You will need to bargain. Tell auto-rickshaw drivers which beaches you want to get to in advance, otherwise they will charge much more when you get there.

Taxi Prepaid taxis from the airport charge around Rs 350 to Kovalam. From outside Mascot Hotel taxis charge about Rs 7 per km; to **Kovalam**, Rs 175, return Rs 225 (waiting: extra Rs 50 per hr). From outside train station, Rs 5 per km. To **Kanniyakumari** with a stop at Padmanabhapuram costs about Rs 900/1100.

Train Central Station, T132. Reservations in building adjoining station. Advance, upstairs, open 0700-1300, 1330-1930, Sun 0900-1700; ask to see Chief Reservations Supervisor, Counter 8. **Kochi (Ernakulam)** (5¼ hrs), via **Varkala** and the backwater towns: around 20 trains daily 0500-2145 including: *Kerala Exp 12625*, 1115; and *Trivandrum Ernakulam Exp 16342*, 1710. **Bengaluru**: *Island Exp 16525*, 1255, 18 hrs. **Mangalore**: *Parasuram Exp 16650*, 0630, 14 hrs; and *Malabar Exp 16629*, 1830, via **Kochi, Thrissur, Kozhikode** and **Kannur. Chennai**: *TVC Chennai Exp 12696*, 1710, 15 hrs. **Kanniyakumari**: *Kanyakumari Jayanti Exp 16381*, 1020, 2½ hrs.

Kovalam and nearby resorts *p33, map p34*
There are 3 main points of access to Kovalam's beaches. Remember to specify which when hiring an auto or taxi.
Bus Local: Frequent buses depart 0540-2100 to East Fort, **Thiruvananthapuram**, from bus stand outside **Ashok Hotel** gate on Kovalam Beach (30 mins, Rs 9). From East Fort bus station, walk or catch an auto-rickshaw to town centre (Rs 20).
Long distance: To **Kanniyakumari, Kochi** via **Kollam (Quilon)** and **Kottayam, Nagercoil, Padmanabhapuram, Varkala** and **Thodopuzha** via **Kottayam**.

Rickshaw Auto-rickshaw to **Thiruvananthapuram**, Rs 70-80, but bargain hard.

Taxi From taxi stand or through Ashok or Samudra hotels. One-way to **Thiruvananthapuram** or airport, Rs 200; station Rs 175; city sights Rs 600; **Kanniyakumari, Padmanabhapuram**, Rs 1750 (8 hrs); **Kochi**, Rs 2250 (5 hrs); **Kollam**, Rs 1100; **Thekkady**, Rs 2650 (6 hrs).

Varkala *p36, map p36*
Bus To/from **Temple Junction** (not beach) for **Alappuzha** and **Kollam**, but often quicker to go to Paripally on NH47 and catch onward buses from there.

Motorcycle Kovalam Motorcycle hire, Voyager Travels, Eye's Beach Rd, T0471-248 1993. Next door to **JA Tourist Home**, Temple Junction; and **Mamma Chompo**, Beach Rd.

Rickshaw/taxi Autos and taxis can be found on Beach Rd and near the helipad. Both charge about Rs 50 to train station. Taxi to **Thiruvananthapuram**, Rs 1000 (1¼ hrs).

Train Varkala sits on the Kochi–Trivandrum line, with at least 20 trains a day in each direction. All northbound trains call at **Kollam**, while many of the southbound trains continue to **Kanniyakumari**.

● Directory

Thiruvananthapuram *p31, map p32*
Banks Mon-Fri 1000-1400, Sat 1000-1200. Most banks can be found on MG Rd including **Andhra Bank, Canara Bank** and **State Bank of India**. All have ATMs. The airport has banks and money exchange facilities including **Thomas Cook**, T0471-250 2470. **Medical services** Many chemists, near hospitals; a few near Statue Junction. Opticians: **Lens & Frames**, Pulimudu Junction, T0471-247 1354. **General Hospital**, Vanchiyoor, T0471-230 7874, **Ramakrishna Ashrama Hospital**, Sasthamangalam, T0471-272 2125, **Cosmopolitan Hospital**, T0471-244 8182 and **Vrindavan Ayurvedic Health Centre**, Kumarapuram, T0471-244 0376. **Useful contacts** Foreigners' Regional Registration Office, City Police Commissioner, Residency Rd, Thycaud, T0471-232 0579; allow up to a week for visas, though it can take less. Mon-Sat 1000-1700. **Wildlife Warden**, PTP Nagar, Vattiyoorkavu, T0471-236 0762.

Kovalam and nearby resorts *p33, map p34*
Banks Canara Bank, ICICI Bank, both at Kovalam Junction; ATMs. **Catholic Syria Bank**, Kovalam Beach Rd, has an ATM. **Central Bank**, branch in Kovalam Hotel (around the corner near the bookshop) changes money and TCs for non-residents after 1045, T0471-248 0101. Nearly all tour operators and many hotels offer money exchange. Best rates, however, are at the airport. **Wilson's**, T0471-248 1647, changes money, any time, no hassle. **Internet** Several on Lighthouse Beach. **Medical services** Emergency assistance either through your hotel or from **Government Hospital** in Thiruvananthapuram. **Upasana Hospital**, near *Le Meridien* gate, T0471-248 0632, has experienced English-speaking doctor.

Varkala *p36, map p36*
Banks State Bank of India, Temple Junction has an ATM. There are several money changers: along the north cliff and around Temple Junction (lower than US$/£ rate at Trivandrum airport), and most will give cash advances on credit cards (at a hefty 5% commission).

Backwaters

Kerala is synonymous with its lyrical backwaters: a watery cat's cradle of endlessly intersecting rivers, streams, lagoons and tanks that flood the alluvial plain between the Indian Ocean and Western Ghats. They run all the way from Kollam via Alappuzha and Kottayam to Kochi to open up a charming slow-tempo window onto Keralite waterfront life: this is the state's lush and fertile Christian belt, Arundhati Roy country, with lakes fringed by bird sanctuaries, idyllic little hamlets, beside huge paddy ponds rustling in the breeze.

The silent daybreak is best, as boats cut through the mist, geese and ducks start to stir along banks, plumes from breakfast fires drift out across the lagoons. As the hamlets and villages wake, Kerala's domestic scene comes to life: clothes are pounded clean, teeth brushed, and smartly turned out primary school children swing their ways to class.

Luxury houseboats are the quintessential way of seeing the waterfront, but they can be shocking polluters, and if your budget or attention span won't stretch that far the state-operated ferries will give you much the same access for a fraction of the fee. Alternatively, borrow a bicycle or move around by car; the roads and canals are interchangeable. Both thread their way through flood plains the size of football pitches, brown lakes with new shoots prodding out and netted fields that protect prawns and fish from snooping white egrets. At dusk young men sit about on bridges or congregate by teashops made of corrugated iron, while others shimmy up coconut palms to tap a fresh supply of sour moonshine toddy, and kids catch fish with poles.

Arriving in the backwaters

Getting there and around   The chief embarkation point for houseboat trips through the backwaters is **Alappuzha** (Alleppey), 64 km south of Kochi on the shore of Lake Vembanad. Trains pull in at the station 3 km west of the town centre, while the bus stand is right on the waterfront, a short walk from several budget hotels and the main houseboat jetty. The other main centres are **Kumarakom**, across the lake from Alappuzha and a short taxi ride from the railway station at Kottayam; and **Kollam**, 70 km north of Trivandrum on the southern end of Lake Ashtamudi, linked to Alappuzha by road, rail and ferry.

Buses, trains and taxis link the main backwaters towns, but the most appealing ways to explore are by bike and boat. A cheap alternative to the full houseboat experience is to spend a few hours riding the ferries that ply across Lake Vembanad and south to Kollam. The 'tourist boat' from Alappuzha to Kollam gives you eight hours on the water at a bargain price of Rs 300, but it's a long day and lacks the peace of the best houseboats. ▶ *See Transport, page 60.*

Tourist information   In Kollam: **District Tourism Promotion Council (DTPC)** ⓘ *Govt Guest House Complex, T0474-275 0170; also at DTPC bus station, T0474-274 5625, train station and ferry jetty, www.dtpckollam.com*, offers cruises, coach tours, and details of *Kathakali* performances. In Alappuzha: **KTDC** ⓘ *Motel Araam, T0477-224 4460*; **ATDC**, *Komala Rd, T0477-226 4462, info@atdcalleppey.com*; **DTPC** ⓘ *KSRTC bus station near jetty, T0477-225 3308, 0830-2000*, is helpful and offers good backwaters trips. In Kottayam: **tourist office** ⓘ *Government Guest House, Nattakom, T0481-256 2219*. In Kumarakom: **Responsible Tourism Travel Desk** ⓘ *T0481-252 4343*, books tours to meet local craftsmen.

Kollam (Quilon) → *For listings, see pages 55-61. Phone code: 0474. Population 361,400.*

Kollam is a busy shaded market town on the side of the Ashtamudi Lake and the headquarters of India's cashew nut trading and processing industry. It is congested and there's little reason to linger, but its position at the south end of Kerala's backwaters, where the waterways are less crowded than those further north, make it a good alternative starting point for boat trips up the canals. ▶ *See What to do, page 59.*

Known to Marco Polo as 'Koilum', the port saw trading between Phoenicians, Persians, Greeks, Romans and Arabs as well as the Chinese. Kollam became the capital of the Venad Kingdom in the ninth century. The educated king Raja Udaya Marthanda Varma convened a special council at Kollam to introduce a new era. After extensive astronomical calculations the new era was established to start on 15 August AD 825. The town was associated with the early history of Christianity.

From the KSWTC boat jetty in the city centre you can hire houseboats or sightseeing boats (a houseboat in appearance but with large seating areas instead of bedrooms) to explore the palm-fringed banks of **Ashtamudi Lake**. You might see Chinese fishing nets and large-sailed dugouts carrying the local crops of coir, copra and cashew. **Munroe Island** is a popular destination for tours, with coir factories, good birdwatching and narrow canals to explore.

Kollam to Alappuzha → *Backwater tours: A ferry leaves for Alappuzha at 1030 (8 hrs).*
Mata Amritanandamayi Ashram ⓘ *10 km north of Kollam at Vallikkavua, accessible by boat or road (through Kayambkulam or Karungappally), www.amritapuri.org, Rs 150 per day*, a giant, pink skyscraper sandwiched on the backwaters between the sea and the river, is the

Kerala backwaters

ashram of 'Amma' (the hugging 'Mother'). Thousands, Western and Indian alike, attend *Darshan* in hope of a hug. The ashram feels a bit lacklustre when Amma is on tour. She has hugged around three million people so far. In the early days, these used to last for minutes; now she averages one hug every 1½ seconds, so she can happily hug 30,000 in a day. The ashram has shops, a bank, library and internet. Smoking, sex and alcohol are forbidden.

Mannarsala, 32 km before Alappuzha, has a tremendously atmospheric **Nagaraja Temple** buried deep in a dense jungle forest. Traditionally *naga* (serpent) worshippers had temples in serpent groves. Mannarsala is the largest of these in Kerala with '30,000 images' of snake gods lined up along the path and among the trees, and many snakes living around the temple. Childless women come for special blessing and also return for a 'thanksgiving' ceremony afterwards when the child born to the couple is placed on special scales and gifts in kind equalling the weight are donated. The temple is unusual for its chief priestess.

The village of **Haripad** has one of Kerala's oldest and most important **Subrahmanya temples**. The four-armed idol is believed to have been found in a river, and in August the three-day **Snake Boat Race** at Payipad, 3 km by bus, commemorates its rescue and subsequent building of the temple. There are boat processions on the first two days followed by competitive races on the third day. There is a guesthouse on **Mankotta Island** on the backwaters; the large comfortable rooms with bath are well kept.

Where to stay 🛏
Anthraper Home Stay **1**
Coconut Palms **9**
Emerald Isle
  Heritage Villa **7**
Keraleeyan Lakeside
  Ayurvedic Resort **3**
Marari Beach &
  Marari Beach Home **4**
Mata Amritanandamayi
  Ashram **10**
Olavipe **5**
Poopally's Heritage
  Homestay **6**
Purity **2**
Vembanad House
  Homestay **8**

Squeezed between the backwaters and the sea, and 12 km from Haripad station, **Thottapally** makes a good stop on a backwaters trip, two hours from Alappuzha.

About 10 km from Chengannur, **Aranmula** has the Parthasarathi Temple and is known for its unique metal mirrors. The **Vallamkali (or Utthrittathi) festival** on the last day of Onam (August-September) is celebrated with a boat race. The festival celebrates the crossing of the river by Krishna, who is believed to be in all the boats simultaneously, so the challenge is to arrive at the same time, rather than race.

Alappuzha (Alleppey) and around → *For listings, see pages 55-61. Phone code: 0477. Population: 177,100.*

Alappuzha (pronounced *Alappoorra*) has a large network of canals, choked with the blue flowers of water hyacinth, passing through the town. It's the chief departure point for cruises into the backwaters and the venue for the spectacular **snake boat races** (see Festivals, page 59). **Houseboat trips** can be arranged at any of the numerous tour operators in town or directly, by heading to the boat dock just off VCNB Road. Although the town itself doesn't have many tourist sites, it's a pleasant, bustling place to walk around and there's a lovely stretch of undeveloped beach as well.

Alappuzha (Alleppey)

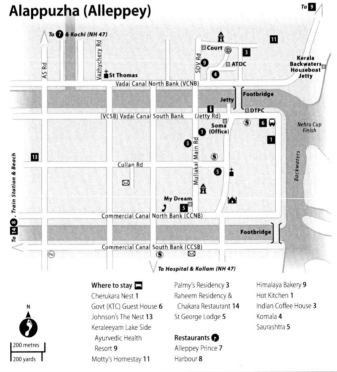

Where to stay 🛏
Cherukara Nest **1**
Govt (KTC) Guest House **6**
Johnson's The Nest **13**
Keraleeyam Lake Side
  Ayurvedic Health
  Resort **9**
Motty's Homestay **11**

Palmy's Residency **3**
Raheem Residency &
  Chakara Restaurant **14**
St George Lodge **5**

Restaurants 🍴
Alleppey Prince **7**
Harbour **8**

Himalaya Bakery **9**
Hot Kitchen **1**
Indian Coffee House **3**
Komala **4**
Saurashtra **5**

Preserving the backwaters for the future

The backwaters are lagoons fed by a network of perennial rivers with only two permanent outlets to the sea. The salts are flushed out between May and September, but sea waters rush inland by up to 20 km at the end of the monsoon and the waters become increasingly brackish through the dry season. This alternation between fresh and salt water has been essential to the backwaters' aquatic life. However, as land value has rocketed and reclamation for agriculture has reduced the surface water area, the backwaters' fragile ecology has been put at risk. Many of the original swamps have been destroyed and the waters are becoming increasingly saline.

Tourism, too, is taking its toll. Exploring the backwaters in a traditional *kettuvallam* is the ultimate Kerala experience but the popularity of these trips is having an adverse effect on the waterways. However, there are ways to help prevent further degeneration.

The trend so far has been for houseboat operators to offer larger, more luxurious boats (some even equipped with plunge pools) to meet the demands of tourists. The powerful outboard motors contribute heavily to pollution levels in the canals. Opting for a smaller boat not only helps ease environmental damage but also allows you to venture into the many narrower and less visited lagoons that the larger boats are unable to access.

Some operators are becoming aware of the damage being caused and are putting responsible travel practices in place. Support these efforts by checking that your houseboat is equipped with a chemical toilet (to prevent your waste being dumped into the canals) and if possible, opting for a solar-powered boat. Alternatively consider hiring a hand-propelled *thoni* or canoe as an entirely carbon neutral way of exploring this unique region.

Mararikulam, 15 km north of Alappuzha on the coast, is a quiet, secluded beach which, until recently, was only known to the adjoining fishing village. The main village has a thriving cottage industry of coir and jute weaving.

Some 16 km southeast of Alappuzha is the hushed backwaters village of **Champakulam** where the only noise pollution is the odd squeak of a bicycle and the slush of a canoe paddle. The Syrian Christian church of **St Mary's Forane** was built in 1870 on the site of a previous church dating from AD 427. The English-speaking priest is happy to show visitors round. Nearby the **St Thomas Statuary** makes wooden statues of Christ for export round the world: a 2-m-tall Jesus will set you back US$450. To get there, take the Alappuzha–Changanacherry bus (every 30 minutes) to Moncombu (Rs 4), then an auto-rickshaw to Champakulam (4 km, Rs 12). Alternatively the Alappuzha–Edathna ferry leaves at 0615 and 1715 and stops at Champakulam. In the backwater village of **Edathna**, you can visit the early Syrian **St George's Church**.

Kottayam and Kumarakom → *For listings, see pages 55-61. Phone code: 0481.*
Population: 60,700.

Around Kottayam lies some of the lushest and most beautiful scenery in the state, with hills to its east and backwaters to its west. Kottayam itself is the capital of Kerala's Christian community, which belonged to the Orthodox Syrian tradition up till the Portuguese arrival. Two churches of the era survive 2 km north of town, in the 450-year-old **Cheria Palli** ('Small' St Mary's Church), which has beautiful vegetable dye mural paintings over its altar, and the **Valia Palli** ('Big' St Mary's Church), from 1550, with two Nestorian crosses carved on plaques behind two side altars. One has a Pallavi inscription on it, the other a Syriac. The cross on the left of the altar is the original and may be the oldest Christian artefact in India; the one to the right is a copy. By the altar there is an unusual small triptych of an Indian St George slaying a dragon. Note the interesting Visitors' Book (1898-1935); a paper cutting reports that "the church has attracted many European and native gentlemen of high position". Mass at Valia Palli at 0900 on Sunday, and Cheria Palli at 0730 on Sunday and Wednesday. The Malankara Syrian Church has its headquarters at Devalokam.

Ettumanoor, just north of Kottayam, has possibly the wealthiest temple in Kerala. The present Mahadeva temple was constructed in 1542, and is famous for its murals depicting scenes from the *Ramayana* and the Krishna legends, both inside and outside the *gopuram*. The typical circular shrine with a copper-covered conical roof encloses a square sanctuary. The **Arattu festival** in March draws thousands of pilgrims when gold elephant statues are displayed. They weigh 13 kg each.

Tucked among the waterways of Vembanad Lake, in mangrove, paddy and coconut groves with lily-studded shores, is **Kumarakom**, 16 km from Kottayam. Here are stacks of exclusive hotels where you can be buffed and Ayurvedically preened, bent into yoga postures, peacefully sunbathe or take to the water: perfect honeymoon territory.

The tourism department has developed an old rubber plantation set around Vembanad Lake into a **bird sanctuary** ① *1000-1800*. A path goes through the swamp to the main bird nesting area. **Pathiramanal** ('midnight sands') **Island** in the middle of the lake can be reached by boat. The best season for birdlife is June-August; to visit in the early morning.

Backwaters listings

For hotel and restaurant price codes and other relevant information, see pages 14-17.

● Where to stay

Kollam (Quilon) *p50*
$$$$ Fragrant Nature Retreat and Resorts, Paravur, T0474-251 4000, www.fragrantnature. com. A 4-star luxury lakeside resort with spa, swimming pool and jacuzzi. Accommodation in lakeside rooms or villas.
$$$ Aquasserenne, Paravoor, 15 mins from town by road or boat, T0474-251 2410, www.aquasserenneindia.com. Splendid backwaters location, well-furnished chalets (some reassembled Kerala houses) with TV, restaurant, Ayurvedic massage/treatment, boat rides.
$$$-$$ Valiyavila Family Estate, Panamukkam Jetty, Kureepuzha, access by ferry (frequent, Rs 3) from Kollam boat jetty, T0474-270 1546, www.kollamlakeviewresort. com. 6 bright, breezy rooms in large house right on the lakeside. Peaceful location, lovely garden with hammocks, great views. Friendly, attentive staff. Wide selection of meals available. Eccentric 55-ft statue of 'Goddess of Light' in garden means you can't miss this place. Good discounts off-season. Canoe trips. Recommended.
$$ Nani, opposite Clock Tower, Chinnakada, T0474-275 1141, www.hotelnani.com. Swish business hotel close to the railway station, with smart if slightly overpriced rooms and friendly staff.
$$-$ Tamarind (KTDC), Ashramam, T0474-274 5538, www.ktdc.com/tamarind. Newly renovated rooms in a bland block building. All rooms with a/c, TV. Nice views of the waterway. Quiet location, restaurant, boat hire.
$ Government Guest House, Ashramam, T0474-274 3620. Live like the British Raj on a pauper's budget. 12 simply furnished rooms, all with attached bath, in the sprawling former residence of the British governor.

More expensive rooms have bathrooms large enough to throw a party in. High ceilings, shady veranda, huge garden, bags of character, friendly staff. Some cheaper rooms are in bland modern building at the back. Meals on request. Recommended.
$ Mahalaxmi Lodge, opposite bus station, T0474-276 3823. Smallish, moderately clean, basic rooms, some with attached bath and TV.

Kollam to Alappuzha *p50, map p51*
$$-$ Coconut Palms, Kumarakodi, T0471-301 8100, www.coconutpalms.co.in. Idyllic 200-year-old traditional house in shaded compound, on backwaters and 100 m from sea. Yoga, Ayurveda and package deals available.
$ Mata Amritanandamayi Ashram, Vallikkavu, T0476-289 6399, www.amritapuri. org. Amma's ashram offers spartan but spacious accommodation in a multi-storey block, with hugs and South Indian meals included in the price. Western canteen (at extra cost) serves American-style meals.

Alappuzha (Alleppey) and around *p52, maps p51 and p52*
Book ahead to avoid the scramble off the ferry. Hotels north of Vadai Canal are quieter.
$$$$ Marari Beach, Mararikulam, Alappuzha, T0478-286 3801, www.cghearth. com. Well-furnished, comfortable, local-style cottages (garden villas, garden pool villas and 3 deluxe pool villas) in palm groves – some with private pool. Good seafood, pool, Ayurvedic treatment, yoga in the morning, *pranayama* in the evening, shop, bikes, badminton, beach volleyball, boat cruises (including overnight houseboat), farm tours, friendly staff, discounts Apr-Sep. Recommended.
$$$$ Motty's Homestay, Kidangamparambu Rd, Alappuzha, T(0)9847-032836, motty@alleppeybeach.com. Just 2 double rooms, with old furniture and 4-poster

beds, in a private house on Alappuzha's outskirts. Excellent home-cooked breakfast and dinner included.

$$$$ Olavipe, Thekanatt Parayil, Olavipe, 25 km from Kochi, T0478-252 2255, www.olavipe. com. Century-old mansion belonging to family of Syrian Christan notables, on a 16-ha organic farm on the lush island of Olavipe. 5 rooms: 3 in the main house and 2 in a cottage.

$$$$ Purity, Muhamma, Aryakkara, (8 km from Alappuzha town), T0484-221 6666, www.malabarhouse.com. This beautiful Italianate villa, set on an acre of tropical grounds overlooking Lake Vembanad, is the most elegant lodging for miles around, with minimalist decor and a smattering of rare antiques. Huge rooms on the ground floor open out to a grassy lawn, but for the ultimate splurge check in to the huge turquoise-toned suite upstairs, with arched windows hoovering up views of the glassy lake. There's a pool and a discreet spa offering Ayurvedic treatments and yoga classes, and high class dinners, which the chef can tailor to your wishes, are served around a pond in the courtyard. Superb in every respect and thoroughly recommended.

$$$$ Raheem Residency, Beach Rd, Alappuzha, T0477-223 9767, www.raheemresidency.com. Special luxury heritage hotel housed in a beautifully restored colonial 19th-century bungalow, on a pristine piece of Kerala's coast. 10 immaculate rooms, all with a/c and lovely antique furnishings. Palatial living room, jasmine-scented garden, excellent restaurant and a lovely pool under a velvet apple tree. The Irish journalist owner also offers the property as a writers' retreat (contact for prices). Easily the best address in Alappuzha. Recommended.

$$$$-$$$ Anthraper Home Stay, Cherthala, T0478-281 3211, www.anthrapergardens.com. Charming country house on the backwaters. Sprawling garden, cooking demonstrations, yoga, canoeing, fishing and river walks.

$$$$-$$$ Emerald Isle Heritage Villa, Kanjooparambil-Manimalathan, T0477-270 3899, www.emeraldislekerala.com. 4 rooms on the shores of an island of lush jungle, surrounded by sunken paddy field. Toddy on tap, cookery courses, boat trips, Ayurveda. The magic of the place begins on the 10-km journey from Alappuzha.

$$$ Pooppally's Heritage Homestay, Pooppally Junction, Nedumudy, T0477-276 2034, www.pooppallys.com. Traditional wooden cottage (water bungalow) and rooms, with open-air bathrooms, in 19th-century family farmhouse, shaded by a mango tree, set in a garden stretching down to the River Pampa. Great home-cooked food. Catch the ferry to Alappuzha for 90 mins of free houseboat.

$$$ Vembanad House Homestay, Puthankayal, Alappuzha, T0478-286 8696, www.vembanadhouse.com. 4 spacious rooms in stately heritage house surrounded by a lake in the pretty Muhamma area. Fresh food from the family farm cooked to Kerala recipes. Traditional architecture with modern bathrooms (no a/c). The house is managed by the delightful Balakrishnan family.

$$ Keraleeyam Lakeside Ayurvedic Health Resort, off Thathampally main road, Alappuzha, T0477-223 1468, www.keraleeyam.com. Keraleeyam sits on one of the prettiest nubs of the backwaters and is one of the most reasonable places to embark on a proper Ayurvedic programme. Doctors attend daily, there's no alcohol, and the menu is tailored according to your Ayurvedic body type. Cottages on the lake are better than the drab rooms in the main house.

$$-$ Cherukara Nest, just around the corner from KSRTC bus station, Alappuzha, T0477-225 1509, www.cherukaranest.com. Airy, cool, spotlessly clean rooms in a peaceful traditional family home. Rattan furniture on large shady porches. Pigeon house in the back garden. Very helpful and friendly. Meals available on request.

$ Government Guest House (KTDC), Jetty Rd, Alappuzha, T0477-224 4460. Bright yellow building next door to the KSRTC bus station. More expensive rooms are large but have tired-looking bathrooms. Cheaper bamboo-walled rooms on 3rd floor. Be careful not to trip over the staff members fast asleep on the veranda. Free bike hire, internet.

$ Johnson's The Nest, Lal Bagh Factory Ward (West of Convent Sq), Alappuzha, T0477-224 5825, www.johnsonskerala.com. Friendly family-run guesthouse in a quiet street away from the town centre. 6 rooms, each with balcony. Free pick-up from bus station, internet, houseboat facility, popular.

$ Palmy's Residency, north of new Matha footbridge, Alappuzha, T0477-223 5938, www.palmyresidency.com. Large, clean rooms with fly-screens and fans. Quiet but central location. More expensive rooms have big balconies to lounge in. Local waterway canoe trips (4-5 hrs, Rs 200 per hr). Free bike hire. Recommended.

$ St George Lodge, CCNB Rd, Alappuzha, T0477-225 1620. Don't let the dilapidated façade put you off – this is an excellent cheapie. 80 very basic but clean rooms, some with attached bath. Friendly staff.

Kottayam and Kumarakom p54

In Kumarakom 26% taxes are added to bills.

$$$$ Coconut Lagoon, Vembanad Lake Kumarakom (CGH Earth), T0484-301 1711, www.cghearth.com. Comfortable heritage *tharavads* (traditional Keralite wooden cottages), heritage mansions and pool villas. Outdoor restaurant facing lagoon, good dinner buffet, pool, yoga, very friendly, Ayurvedic treatments, attractive waterside location, spectacular approach by boat (10 mins from road). Vechoor cows mow the lawns. Recommended. Discounts Apr-Sep.

$$$$ Philipkutty's Farm, Pallivathukal, Ambika Market, Vechoor, Kottayam, T0482-

927 6529, www.philipkuttysfarm.com. 5 immaculate waterfront villas sharing an island on Vembanad Lake. The delightful working farm boasts coconut, banana, nutmeg, coca and vanilla groves. Delicious home cooking and personal attention from all the family. No a/c or TV. Cooking and painting holidays.

$$$$ Privacy at Sanctuary Bay, Kannamkara, opposite Kumarakom, T0484-221 6666, www.malabarhouse.com. Absolute lakeside isolation in a fully-staffed but fully self-contained 3-bedroom bungalow. Modern opulent interiors hide behind the old Keralite facade, and there's stunning veranda looking out across the lake.

$$$$ Vivanta by Taj, Kumarakom, T0481-252 5711, www.vivantabytaj.com. 19 a/c rooms, in sensitively renovated 120-year-old 'Bakers' House', as featured in *The God of Small Things*. Also newer cottages and a moored houseboat, good meals. An intimate hotel but packed.

$$$$ Waterscapes (KTDC), Kumarakom, T0481-252 5861. Idyllic cottage experience on the backwaters. All chalets have a/c and cable TV. Pool, bar, restaurant.

$$ GK's Riverview Homestay, Valliadu, Aymanam, T0481-259 7527, www.gk homestay-kumarakom.com. Set amid paddy fields in the heart of *God of Small Things* country, George and Dai's lovely house offers home comforts in the shape of simple immaculate rooms, hammocks lazily overlooking the river, and superb Kerala cooking. The consummate hosts are always on hand to share secrets of the area, and arrange excellent tours.

$$-$ Aida, MC Rd, 2 km from railway, Kottayam, T0481-256 8391, www. hotelaidakerala.com. Clean, pleasant rooms with bath, some with a/c. Front rooms can be noisy. Restaurant, bar, helpful staff.

$$-$ Anjali Park, KK Rd, 4 km from railway, Kottayam, T0481-256 3661. Decent rooms with bath and a/c. Good restaurants.

$ Ambassador Hotel, KK Rd (set back), T0481-256 3293. Friendly Indian-style hotel with good restaurant and bar. Very good value.

$ Green Park, Kurian Uthup Rd, Nagampadam, T0481-256 3331, greenparkhotel@yahoo.co.in. Adequate rooms with bath. A/c rooms noisy, non-a/c at back too hot. Restaurant.

$ Kaycee's Residency, off YMCA Rd, Kottayam, T0481-256 3440. Good value, clean, decent-sized rooms.

$ PWD Rest House, on hill 2 km south of Kottayam, T0481-256 8147. Remarkable late 19th-century building with superb furniture, overlooking vista of paddy fields.

$ Venad Tourist Complex, Ancheril Building, near State Bus Stand, Kottayam, T0481-258 1383. Modern building with clean rooms. Restaurant. Recommended.

🍴 Restaurants

Kollam (Quilon) *p50*

$ Eat N Pack, near Taluk Office, Main St. Excellent value, clean, good choice of dishes, friendly. Recommended.

$ Indian Coffee House, Main Rd. For good coffee and vegetarian and non-vegetarian South Indian food. Nice waiter service and good atmosphere.

$ Suprabhatam, opposite clock tower, Main St. Adequate vegetarian.

Alappuzha (Alleppey) and around
p52, map p52

$$$ Chakara, Raheem Residency, Beach Rd. Rooftop dining with attentive service and excellent multi-cuisine food. The 4-course set dinner menu (pegged at rupee equivalent to €11) is unbeatable value. Alcohol available.

$$ Alleppey Prince Hotel, AS Rd (NH47), 2 km from town. International, comfortable a/c restaurant, reasonable food, alcohol in bar only.

$ Harbour, Beach Rd. Specializes in seafood, also has Indian and European dishes. Excellent value. Alcohol available. Recommended.

$ Himalaya Bakery, SDV Rd. Large range of sweet and savoury pastries, and other

snacks, to take out or eat in at the tiny seating area.

$ Hot Kitchen, Mullakal Main Rd. Good for *iddli*, *dosa*, *vadai*, etc.

$ Indian Coffee House, Mullakal Main Rd. Good value, tasty non-vegetarian snacks.

$ Komala, Komala Hotel, Zilla Court Ward. Excellent South Indian *thalis* and Chinese.

$ SAS, Jetty Rd. Good South Indian vegetarian and Chinese.

$ Saurashtra, Cullan Rd. Vegetarian, ample helpings on banana leaf, locally popular.

Kottayam and Kumarakom *p54*

The following are in Kottayam. For options in Kumarakom, see hotels in Where to stay.

$$ Aida, MC Rd. Large, uninspired menu. Pleasantly cool 'chilled' drinks may arrive slightly warm.

$$ Green Park, Kurian Uthup Rd. International menu. Reasonable but slow service. Dinner in mosquito-ridden garden (or in own room for guests). Alcohol available.

Near the state bus station

$ Black Stone, T B Rd. Good vegetarian.

$ Milkshake Bar, T B Rd, opposite Blackstone Hotel. 20 flavours.

✿ Festivals

Kollam (Quilon) *p50*

19 Jan Kerala Tourism Boat Race.

Apr Colourful 10-day Vishnu festival in Asram Temple with procession and fireworks.

Aug-Sep Avadayattukotta Temple celebrates a 5-day Ashtami Rohani festival.

Muharram too is observed with processions at the town mosque.

Alappuzha (Alleppey) and around
p52, map p52

For details see www.keralatourism.org.

9-12 Jan Cheruppu is celebrated in the Mullakal Devi Temple with a procession of elephants, music and fireworks.

17-19 Jan Tourism Boat Race.

Jul/Aug DTPC Boat Race (3rd Sat) in the backwaters. **Champakulam Boat Race**, Kerala's oldest, takes place 16-km ferry ride away on 'Moolam' day. The Nehru Trophy, inaugurated in 1952, is the largest **Snake Boat Race** in the state. As many as 40 highly decorated 'snake boats' are rowed by several dozen oarsmen before huge crowds. Naval helicopters do mock rescue operations and stunt flying. Entry by ticket; Rs 125 (Rs 60/75 tickets allow access in to overcrowded and dangerous areas). There are other snake boat races held throughout the year.

⚙ What to do

Kollam (Quilon) *p50*
Tour operators
As well as houseboat trips on traditional *kettuvallams*, there are also the much cheaper options of Kollam–Alappuzha cruises and shorter canal journeys to Munroe Island. The gentle pace and tranquil waterways make these tours very worthwhile, but the heat and humidity may sometimes make overnight stays on houseboats uncomfortable.
DTPC, boat jetty, T0474-275 0170, www. dtpckollam.com. Daily 8-hr backwater cruise from Kollam to Alappuzha; depart 1030 (Rs 300). You can be dropped off halfway at Alumkadavu (Rs 200) or at Vallikkavu for the Ashram (Rs 150). The only stops are for meals; some travellers find the trip a little too long and samey. A good alternative is a canal trip to Munroe Island village; depart 0900,1300 (6 hrs return, Rs 300).

A more expensive option is to hire a *kettuvallam*. For a 1-bed houseboat prices start at Rs 5000 for 8 hrs day trip, Rs 6500 for overnight, to Rs 12,300 for 2 days and 1 night, inclusive of all meals. There are also cruise packages which combine a day cruise with an overnight stay at a backwater resort (Rs 3500).
Southern Backwaters Tour Operators, opposite KRSTC Bus Station, Jetty Rd, Kollam,

T(0)9495-976037, www.southernbackwaters. com. Independent operators. A/c deluxe and standard houseboats for 1- to 3-night packages. Also motorboat cruises and Munroe Island tours.

Alappuzha (Alleppey) and around
p52, map p52
Tour operators
Alappuzha is the starting point of backwater boat trips to Kollam, Changanacherry, Kottayam and Kochi, and everybody you meet seems to have a houseboat to rent. Some find cruising the backwaters of Lake Vembanad utterly idyllic and restful, while for others the sluggish pace of the houseboats – combined with the heavy crowding of the waterways close to Alappuzha – a form of slow torture. Most first-time visitors go for an overnight tour, which is in some ways the worst of all worlds: you're often moored alongside a raft of other boats, you get trotted through the standard tourist 'village' visits (ie shopping trips), and you simply don't have time to get away from the crowds. If you can spare an extra night or more, longer cruises let you get away into the deeper reaches of the backwaters where canal life still continues more or less unmolested by tourism. On the other hand, if you just want a taste of the scenery, a day cruise – or even one of the cheap ferries that ply the lakes and canals – might satisfy you at a fraction of the price of a night on a houseboat.

It's always worth booking in advance during high season, when the theoretical government-set rates (which are printed and displayed in the DTPC booking office at the jetty in Alappuzha) go out the window, and houseboat owners jack the prices up by 50-80%. Houseboats vary widely depending on the number of bedrooms, facilities (some come with a/c, flatscreen TVs and DVD players), quality of food and the crew's level of English. Booking ahead gives you some degree of certainty over the level of luxury you will find; it also allows you to circumvent the persistent dockside touts, whose commissions mean that any discount you can negotiate comes at the cost of corners cut on the trip. If you're coming outside peak season, and don't mind spending a morning scouting around, making a booking on the spot gives you a chance to inspect a number of boats before agreeing on a price.

The following companies are generally at the top end of the market, but offer reliably good (in some cases superb) service.

CGH Earth, T0484-301 1711, Kochi, www.cghearth.com. Runs 'spice boat' cruises in modified *kettuvallams*, which are idyllic if not luxurious: shaded sit-outs, modern facilities including solar panels for electricity, 2 double rooms, limited menu. US$325.

Discovery 1, Malabar House, Fort Kochi, see page 69. **Malabar Escapes'** take on the houseboat is silent and pollutant free. Because it's nimble and trips are for a minimum of 3 nights, it's guaranteed to take you far from the wider watery motorways bigger rice boats ply. 1 bedroom, large bathroom and sitting room plus sun deck. Food is to Malabar House's high standard.

DTPC, Jetty Rd, T0477-225 1796, www.dtpc alappuzha.com. Runs the same 8-hr backwater cruises as its sister office in Kollam, except going the other way. Departs 1030 from Alappuzha ferry jetty (Rs 400). There is also a shorter round-trip to Kumarakom (4 hrs, Rs 200), and canoe trips through local waterways (Rs 200 per hr).

Lakes and Lagoons Tour Co, Punnamada, T0477-226 6842, www.lakeslagoons.com. Solar-powered 2-bed boats. Consistently recommended operator.

Rainbow Cruises, VCNB Rd, opposite jetty, Alappuzha, T0477-226 1375, www.rainbow cruises.in. Solar powered with high safety standards and emergency speedboat support (houseboats have been known to sink).

⊖ Transport

Kollam (Quilon) *p50*
Local auto-rickshaws are plentiful and bikes are available for hire.

Bus Local buses are plentiful. Long distance buses run from the KSRTC station, T0474-275 2008. Buses every 30 mins from 0600 to **Kochi** (3½ hrs, Rs 87) via **Alappuzha** (2 hrs, Rs 55) and other towns on the coast. Buses run 24 hrs to **Thiruvananthapuram**, leaving every 10 mins in the day and every 30 mins during the night (2 hrs, Rs 44). Change at Thiruvananthapuram for **Kovalam**. It is difficult to get to **Varkala** by bus; take the train.

Car To **Alappuzha**, Rs 750, from the bus station.

Ferry Public ferries sail to **Ghuhandapuram** at 0730, 1100, 1330, 1545 and 1745 (1 hr, Rs 5) and then return to Kollam. It's an interesting journey with views of village life and Chinese fishing nets on the way. The 1745 departure lets you enjoy sunset over the waterways.

Train Junction railway station, T131, is about 3 km east of the boat jetty and bus station. There are several trains a day south to **Thiruvananthapuram** including the *Island Exp 16526*, 1335 (1¾ hrs), which continues to **Kanniyakumari** (4¼ hrs).
All the trains stop at **Varkala** (½ hr).

An equal number of trains head north to **Ernakulam (Cochin)** and points beyond, including the *TVC Chennai Exp 12696* (continues to **Chennai**, 15 hrs); and the *Island Exp 16525* (continues to **Bengaluru**, 16 hrs).

Alappuzha (Alleppey) and around
p52, map p52
It is only a 5-min walk between the ferry jetty and the KSRTC bus station despite what many local rickshaw drivers will tell you.

Bus From the KSRTC Bus Station, T0477-225 2501, there are frequent long-distance buses to **Kochi**, 0630-2330 (1½ hrs, Rs 37); **Thiruvananthapuram**, 0600-2000, (4 hrs, Rs 96) via **Kollam** (2 hrs, Rs 55); **Champakulam**, 0515-2000 (45 mins, Rs 10) and **Kottayam**, 0730-1800 (1½ hrs, Rs 30). There are several buses daily to **Coimbatore**, from 0600 (7 hrs, Rs 96).

Car A car with driver from Alappuzha to **Fort Kochi** (65 km) costs Rs 500-600.

Ferry Public ferries, T0477-225 2015, sail to **Kottayam**, 0730, 1000, 1130, 1300, 1430 and 1730 (3 hrs) and **Changanassery**, 1000, 1300 and 1730 (3 hrs). Also frequent services to **Nedumudi** (1 hr).

Train The train station, T0477-225 3965, is on the coastal route from **Trivandrum–Varkala–Kollam–Ernakulam**, 3 km from the jetty. Frequent trains in both directions.

Kottayam and Kumarakom *p54*
Bus The new Private Bus Station is near the railway station. Buses to Alappuzha only leave from the KSRTC Bus Station, 2 km away; local buses to to **Kumarakom Tourist Village** also run frequently from here. There are fast and frequent long-distance buses to **Alappuzha**, every 45 mins (2 hrs, Rs 30); **Thiruvananthapuram**, every 30 mins (4 hrs, Rs 90); **Kochi**, every 30 mins (1½ hrs, Rs 45) and **Kumily**, every hour (4½ hrs, Rs 68). There are 2 evening departures to **Madurai**, 2045 and 2145 (7 hrs, Rs 120) and 5 buses daily head to **Munnar**, 0600-1600 (5 hrs, Rs 100).

Car Car with driver to **Thekkady**, Rs 850, 4 hrs.

Ferry Ferries leave from the Kodimatha Jetty except during the monsoons, when you should head to the Town Jetty 3 km southwest of the train station. Ferries to **Alappuzha**, 0730, 0930, 1130, 1430,1730 (3 hrs). This is an interesting trip but gets very busy in peak season. Other departures include **Champakulam**, 1530 (4 hrs) and **Mannar**, 1430 (3 hrs).

Train Trains run throughout the day, south to **Thiruvananthapuram** via **Kollam** and **Varkala**, and north to Ernakulam and beyond. No trains to Alappuzha, which is on the parallel coastal line.

Directory

Kollam (Quilon) *p50*
Medical services District Hospital, T0474-279 3409. **Post** Head Post Office, Parameswara Nagar. Mon-Sat until 2000, Sun until 1800.

Alappuzha (Alleppey) and around *p52, map p52*
Banks Catholic Syria Bank, Jetty Rd, and State Bank of India, Cullan Rd. Both have ATMs. **Internet** Several places on Mullakal Rd. Net Café, opposite Kidangamparampu Temple, charges Rs 20 per hr. **Medical services** District Hospital, T0477-225 3324. **Post** Off Mullakal Rd.

Kottayam and Kumarakom *p54*
Banks In Kottayam: Banks are clustered around Ghandi Sq on TB and MC Rds including **Bank of India**, MC Rd and **Ing Bank**, TB Rd. Both have ATMs. **Internet** Many places around Ghandi Sq. **Medical services** District Hospital, T0481-256 3651. **Post** MC Rd, 0800-2000, 1400-1730 on holidays.

Fort Kochi and Ernakulam

Charming Fort Kochi (Cochin) is a true one-off in modern Kerala: a layer cake of colonial India, where British parade grounds overlay Portuguese forts, where Dutch palaces slowly crumble into the soil alongside synagogues, where every turn takes you down some romantically fossilized narrow winding street. Despite a tourist invasion that's flooded the lanes with antique shops, internet cafés and shops flogging fisherman trousers, parts of the ramshackle island still feel frozen back in the 15th and 16th centuries, and the huge trees here are so old that their parasitic aphids are as tall as trees themselves. In the southern quarter of Mattancherry, row upon row of wood-fronted doors give glimpses of rice and spice merchants sitting sifting their produce into small 'tasting' bowls. The iconic batwing Chinese fishing nets, first used in the 14th century, stand on the shores of the north fort area, silhouetted against the lapping waters of one of the world's finest natural harbours: a wide bay interrupted by narrow spits of land and coconut-covered islands.

Before arriving in Fort Kochi, however, you have to negotiate the city's modern centre of gravity – grubby, dynamic Ernakulam, a Rs 5 ferry ride and half a world away across the harbour. While Fort Kochi languishes dreamily in the past, its ambitious sibling is expanding outwards and upwards at breakneck pace, propelled by the vast new container terminal on Vallarpadam Island. The first port in India capable of handling the huge container ships that until now have had to berth in Colombo or Singapore, Kochi stands poised to transform India's logistical landscape, and over the next decade this hitherto sleepy southern city will undoubtedly assume a front-and-centre seat in the future of the Indian economy.

Arriving in Fort Kochi and Ernakulam → *For listings, see pages 69-75. Phone code: 0484. Population: 1.15 million (Kochi 596,500, Ernakulam 558,000).*

Getting there

Kochi's mellow little international airport is at Nedumbassery, 36 km northeast of the city centre. The smoothest way into town is to arrange a pick-up from your hotel (Rs 900-1500 depending on type of car and what your hosts feel the market will support). Alternatively, hire a prepaid taxi from the booth after Customs; a transfer to Fort Kochi costs around Rs 800, a little less to downtown Ernakulam. Air-conditioned buses leave the airport for Fort Kochi bus stand, right in the centre next to the Chinese fishing nets, between 0500 and 1900, taking 90 minutes.

Most trains pull into Ernakulam Junction station in the busy city centre. State-run long distance buses arrive at the Central Bus Stand, 500 m north of Ernakulam Junction, while private buses pull in to the terminal at Kaloor Junction about 2 km further north. Local buses, taxis and autorickshaws connect the various transport hubs. A rickshaw from either to the main jetty, for Fort Kochi, costs approximately Rs 25. ▸▸ *See Transport, page 74.*

Getting around

Fort Kochi has all the sights and a huge number of hotels, and many visitors never leave its cozy bubble. The quiet roads are easy to explore on foot or by bicycle, with an occasional cameo from an autorickshaw. If you need to get across to Ernakulam there are two routes: a circuitous trip by bus, taxi or autorickshaw (Rs 250-500), or one of the cheap and cheerful ferries that chug across the harbour to Ernakulam's Main Jetty – an enjoyably breezy 30-minute trip that's most atmospheric around sunset (ferries run 0600 to 2130). From the jetty you can catch a rickshaw to the railway station or bus stand for around Rs 40. Leave plenty of spare time if you need to travel during peak hours. After 2130 public transport begins to grind to a halt and you'll need to take a rickshaw or taxi to get around.

Tourist information

Kerala Tourism Development Corporation (KTDC) ⓘ *Shanmugham Rd, Ernakulam, T0484-235 3234, 0800-1800.* **Tourist Desk** ⓘ *Main Boat Jetty, Ernakulam, T0484-237 1761, and on Tower Rd in Fort Kochi, T0484-221 6129, www.touristdesk.in, 0900-1800.* This travel agent, with good maps and local information, runs daily backwater tours, has information on more than 2000 temple festivals in Kerala, and runs **Costa Malabari** guesthouse (see page 108).

Background

"If China is where you make your money," declared Italian traveller Nicolas Conti in the Middle Ages, "then Kochi surely is the place to spend it." Kochi has acted as a trading port since at least Roman times, and was a link in the main trade route between Europe and China. From 1795 until India's Independence the long outer sand spit, with its narrow beach leading to the wide bay inland, was under British political control. The inner harbour was in Kochi State, while most of the hinterland was in the separate state of Travancore. The division of political authority delayed development of the harbour facilities until 1920-1923, when the approach channel was dredged so ships that could get through the Suez Canal could dock here, opening the harbour to modern shipping.

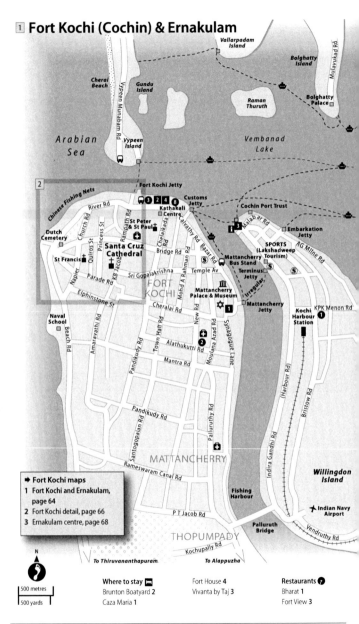

➡ Fort Kochi maps
1 Fort Kochi and Ernakulam,
  page 64
2 Fort Kochi detail, page 66
3 Ernakulam centre, page 68

Where to stay 🛏
Brunton Boatyard 2
Caza Maria 1

Fort House 4
Vivanta by Taj 3

Restaurants 🍴
Bharat 1
Fort View 3

Kayikkas **2**
Seagull **8**

Places in Fort Kochi and Ernakulam

If you land at the Customs Jetty, a plaque in nearby Vasco da Gama Square commemorates the landing of Vasco da Gama in 1500. Next to it is the **Stromberg Bastion**, "one of the seven bastions of Fort Emanuel built in 1767", named after the Portuguese king. Little is left of the 1503 Portuguese fort except ruins. Along the seafront, between the Fort Kochi Bus Stand, the boat jetty and the Dutch cemetery, run the cantilevered Chinese fishing nets. These are not unique to Kochi, but are perhaps uniquely accessible to the short-stay visitor.

Mattancherry Palace and **Parikshith Thampuran Museum** ① *Mattancherry, daily 1000-1700 except Fri and national holidays, Rs 2, photography not allowed*, was first built by the Portuguese around 1557 as a sweetener for the Raja Veera Kerala Varma of Kochi bestowing them trading rights. In 1663, it was largely rebuilt by the new trading power, the Dutch. The layout follows the traditional Kerala pattern known as *nalukettus*, meaning four buildings, which are set around a quadrangle with a temple. There are display cases of the Rajas of Kochi's clothes, palanquins, etc, but these are no match for the amazing murals. The royal bedroom's low wooden walls squeezes the whole narrative of the *Ramayana* into about 45 late 16th-century panels. Every inch is covered with rich red, yellow, black and white. To the south of the Coronation Hall, the *kovinithilam* (staircase room) has six large 18th-century murals including the coronation of Rama. Vishnu is in a room to the north. Two of the women's bedrooms downstairs have 19th-century murals with greater detail. They relate Kalidasa's *Kumarasambava* and themes from the *Puranas*. This stuff is triple x-rated. If you are of a sensitive disposition avert your eyes from panel 27 and 29, whose deer, birds and other animals are captioned as giving themselves up to 'merry enjoyment', a coy way of describing the furious copulation and multiple penetration in plain view. Krishna, meanwhile, finally works out why he was given so many limbs, much to the evident satisfaction of the gopis who are looking on.

The **synagogue** ⓘ *Mattancherry, Sun-Fri 1000-1200, 1500-1700, no video cameras, shoes must be removed*, dating from 1568 (rebuilt in 1662), is near Mattancherry Palace at the heart of what is known as Jew Town, which is a fascinating mixture of shops (some selling antiques), warehouses and spice auction rooms. Stepping inside the synagogue is an extraordinary experience of light and airiness, partly due to the 18th-century blue Cantonese ceramic tiles, hand painted and each one different, covering the floor. There are original glass oil lamps. For several centuries there were two Jewish communities. The earlier group (often referred to as 'black' Jews), according to one source, settled here as early as 587 BC. The earliest evidence of their presence is a copper inscription dated AD 388 by the Prince of Malabar. Those referred to as 'white' Jews came much later, when, with Dutch and then British patronage, they played a major role as trading agents. Speaking fluent Malayalam, they made excellent go-betweens for foreigners seeking to establish

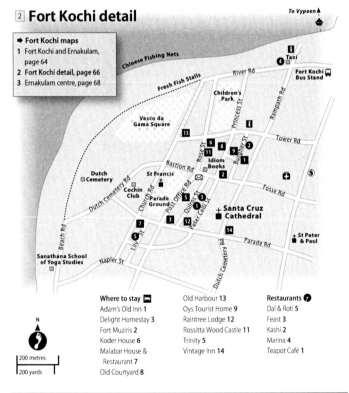

② Fort Kochi detail

➡ Fort Kochi maps
1 Fort Kochi and Ernakulam, page 64
2 Fort Kochi detail, page 66
3 Ernakulam centre, page 68

To Vypeen ▲

Chinese Fishing Nets

Fresh Fish Stalls

River Rd

Fort Kochi Bus Stand

Taxi

Children's Park

Vasco da Gama Square

Princess St

Rampart Rd

Tower Rd

Rose St

Bastion Rd

Burgher St

Idiom Books

Dutch Cemetery

St Francis

Cochin Club

Parade Ground

Church Rd

Post Office Rd

Quiros St

Peter Celli St

Fosse Rd

Santa Cruz Cathedral

+ St Peter & Paul

Beach Rd

Lily St

Napier St

Dutch Cemetery Rd

Parade Rd

Sanathana School of Yoga Studies

N

200 metres
200 yards

Where to stay 🛏	Old Harbour 13	Restaurants 🍴
Adam's Old Inn 1	Oys Tourist Home 9	Dal & Roti 5
Delight Homestay 3	Raintree Lodge 12	Feast 3
Fort Muziris 2	Rossitta Wood Castle 11	Kashi 2
Koder House 6	Trinity 5	Marina 4
Malabar House & Restaurant 7	Vintage Inn 14	Teapot Café 1
Old Courtyard 8		

contacts. The community has shrunk to six families, with many now settled at Moshav Nevatim in Israel's Negev desert. The second Jewish synagogue (in Ernakulam) is deserted.

St Francis' Church ① *Fort Kochi, Mon-Sat 0930-1730, Sun afternoon, Sun services in English 0800 (except for the 3rd Sun of each month)*, was originally dedicated to Santo Antonio, the patron saint of Portugal and is the first church to reflect the new and European-influenced tradition. The original wooden structure (circa 1510) was replaced by the present stone building (there is no authority for the widely quoted date of 1546). Vasco da Gama died on the site in 1524 and was originally buried in the cemetery. Fourteen years later his body was removed to Portugal. The church was renamed St Francis in 1663, and the Dutch both converted it to a Protestant church and substantially modified it. They retained control until 1795, adding the impressive gable façade at the entrance. In 1804, it became an Anglican church. In 1949 the congregation joined the Church of South India. Note the old string-pulled *punkahs* (fans) and the Dutch and Portuguese gravestones that now line the walls.

Santa Cruz Cathedral, near St Francis' Church, originally built in 1557 by the Portuguese, and used as a warehouse by the British in the 18th century, was rebuilt in the early 20th century. It has lovely carved wooden panels and pulpit, and an interesting graveyard.

Museum of Kerala History ① *Ernakulam, 1000-1200 and 1400-1600 except Mon and national holidays*, starts with Neolithic man through St Thomas and Vasco da Gama. Historical personalities of Kerala are represented with sound and light.

Around Fort Kochi and Ernakulam

Bolghatty Island has the 'palace' (circa 1745), set in large gardens and converted into a hotel. It was originally built by the Dutch and then became the home of the British Resident at the court of the Raja of Kochi after 1799. There is still some atmosphere of colonial decay which haunted the old building in its pre-modernized form and gave it much of its charm.

Vypeen Island lies on the northwestern fringe of the harbour. There are quiet beaches here, along with the Portuguese Azhikotta Fort, built around 1503. You can see cannon holes on the walls of the octagonal fort, which was garrisoned by 20 soldiers when it guarded the entrance to the backwaters. Vehicle ferries make the crossing from Fort Kochi.

Our Lady's Convent ① *Palluruthy, Thoppampady, 14 km south, by appointment, T0484-223 0508*, specializes in high-quality needlework lace and embroidery. The sisters are very welcoming and it is an interesting tour with items for sale.

Raksha ① *Yasmin Manzil, VII/370 Darragh-es-Salaam Rd, Kochangadi, T0484-222 7707*, works with children with physical and mental disabilities. Interested volunteers should contact the principal.

Hill Palace Archaeological Museum ① *Thirpunithura, 12 km east of Ernakulam, Tue-Sun 0900-1230, 1400-1700, Rs 11*, has a huge number of historical records and artefacts of the old royal state of Cochin, with portraits, ornaments, porcelain, palm leaf records and ancient musical instruments.

Some 45 km northeast of Kochi is the town of **Kalady**, on the bank of the Periyar River. This popular pilgrimage site was the birthplace of one of India's most influential philosophers, **Sankaracharya**, who lived in the eighth century. He founded the school of *advaita* philosophy, which spread widely across South India. The **Adi Sankara Kirti Stambha Mandapam** ① *0700-1900, small entry fee*, is a nine-storied octagonal tower, 46 m high, and details Sri Sankara's life and works and the Shan Maths, or six ways to

worship. Inside the **Shankara Temple** (Hindus only), are two shrines, one dedicated to
Sankaracharya and the other to the goddess Sarada. The management of the shrines is in
the hands of the Math at Sringeri in Karnataka. Kalady can easily be visited in an afternoon
from Kochi.

③ Ernakulam centre

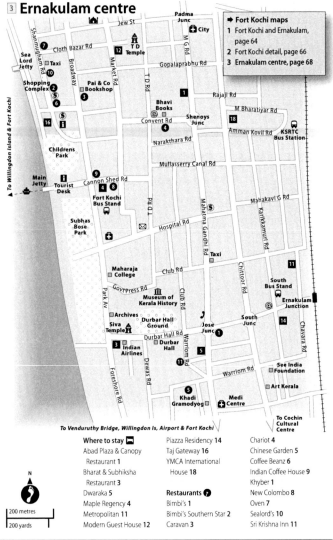

➜ **Fort Kochi maps**
1 Fort Kochi and Ernakulam,
   page 64
2 Fort Kochi detail, page 66
3 Ernakulam centre, page 68

Where to stay 🛏
Abad Plaza & Canopy
   Restaurant **1**
Bharat & Subhiksha
   Restaurant **3**
Dwaraka **5**
Maple Regency **4**
Metropolitan **11**
Modern Guest House **12**

Piazza Residency **14**
Taj Gateway **16**
YMCA International
   House **18**

Restaurants 🍴
Bimbi's **1**
Bimbi's Southern Star **2**
Caravan **3**

Chariot **4**
Chinese Garden **5**
Coffee Beanz **6**
Indian Coffee House **9**
Khyber **1**
New Colombo **8**
Oven **7**
Sealord's **10**
Sri Krishna Inn **11**

Fort Kochi and Ernakulam listings

For hotel and restaurant price codes and other relevant information, see pages 14-17.

🍽 Where to stay

Fort Kochi has bags more character than the busy commercial centre of Ernakulam; book well in advance for the Christmas period.

Fort Kochi *p62, maps p64 and p66*
$$$$ Koder House, Tower Rd, T0484-221 8485, www.koderhouse.com. Boutique hotel in a striking heritage town house formerly owned by prominent Jewish family, and sometime home to ambassadors and heads of state. Luxury suites have huge bedrooms, sitting room, bathroom and jacuzzi. Tiny plunge pool in the back courtyard, spa with massage and facials, plus valet, business centre, superb home-cooked food.
$$$$ Malabar House, 1/268 Parade Rd, near St Francis' Church, T0484-221 6666, www.malabarhouse.com. Fort Kochi's original boutique hotel, and still one of its best. Big and beautiful high-ceilinged rooms in a sensitively restored 18th-century mansion, set around a flagstoned courtyard with an excellent restaurant and small swimming pool. Helpful staff, reliable airport pick-ups and a funky bar make this a perfect if pricey first place to hang your hat.
$$$$ Old Harbour, Tower Rd, T0484-221 8006, www.oldharbourhotel.com. Impeccably restored, 300-year-old Portuguese and Dutch building slap on the harbour front. Rooms have private balconies, some with harbour views. Large garden plus swimming pool, Wi-Fi, Ayurveda, jacuzzi.
$$$$ Trinity, 1/658 Ridsdale Rd, Parade Ground, T0484-221 6669, www.malabarhouse.com. Ultra-modern, minimalist and modish 3-bedroom apartment with airy bathrooms, spacious sitting/dining room, mezzanine, tiny swimming pool. Service is immaculate,

food is at **Malabar House** on the other side of the parade ground.
$$$$ Vivanta by Taj, Willingdon Island, T0484-664 3000, www.vivantabytaj.com. Large, swish hotel overlooking the harbour, with beautifully renovated rooms, the usual superb Taj service. Pool, spa, gym and 5 bars and restaurants.
$$$$-$$$ Brunton Boatyard, Calvathy Rd, T0484-301 1711, www.cghearth.com. Easily the best address in Fort Kochi, adjacent to the Chinese fishing nets on the edge of the Arabian Sea. 18 characterful rooms and 4 deluxe suites, each of which overlooks the harbour in an elegantly restored original boatyard and merchant's house built around a courtyard with a giant rain-tree. Generous swimming pool. Discounts Apr-Sep.
$$$ Fort House, 2/6A Calvathy Rd, T0484-221 7103, www.hotelforthouse.com. Tidy bungalows set in a quiet walled courtyard with its own little jetty. Some rooms charmingly old fashioned, others made from bamboo. Newer, more expensive rooms have modern baths, but they're pretty spartan for the price. Good restaurant overlooking the water.
$$$ Old Courtyard, 1/371 Princess St, T0484-221 6302, www.oldcourtyard.com. Beautiful, comfortable rooms, superbly styled with old wooden furniture, overlooking large, breezy courtyard of pretty pot plants and sit-outs. The suite is easily the most romantic with a 4-poster bed and white cotton. Attentive liveried staff, breakfast included, average food but excellent cakes and Turkish coffee, and lovely calm atmosphere. Recommended.
$$$-$$ Rossitta Wood Castle, Rose St, T0484-221 5671, www.rossittawoodcastle.com. 300-year-old Dutch mansion. Rooms, with quirky features and lots of wood-panelling, set around an open-air restaurant courtyard. Breakfast included. Art gallery, library internet café, spa, hot water, yoga.

$$ Caza Maria Hotel, 6/125 Jew Town Rd, Mattancherry, T0484-395 8837, cazamaria@ rediffmail.com. Just 2 huge and wonderful rooms in beautiful converted house, with tiled floors, wooden furniture and antiques: isolated (the only hotel in Jew Town), romantic and shabbily elegant. Fan only. Breakfast is included, at French/Indian restaurant of same name (on the opposite side of the street). Highly recommended.

$$ Raintree Lodge, Petercelli St, T0484-325 1489, www.fortcochin.com. Friendly little lodge in quiet location. Large clean rooms all with hot water and a/c. Pretty roof terrace to relax on.

$$-$ Delight Homestay, Parade Ground, Ridsdale Rd, T0484-221 7658. This lovingly restored Portuguese provides a welcoming peaceful haven. Airy, spotlessly clean rooms open onto a wide terrace, budget rooms are great value. The garden is a riot of colourful blooms. Breakfast is served at the family table. A home away from home. Highly recommended.

$$-$ Fort Muziris, 1/415 Burgar St, T0484-221 5057, www.fortmuziris.com. Friendly backpacker refuge in the centre of things. The pick of the rooms are the upstairs suites with kitchen and shared terrace.

$ Adam's Old Inn, CC1/430 Burgher St, T0484-221 7595. Popular budget-traveller haunt in restored old building. Dorm beds are available for Rs 150. Helpful manager.

$ Oy's Tourist Home, Burgher St, T099-4759 4903. Decent rooms in lovely lamp-lit old building, with lots of plants. Can be noisy.

$ Vintage Inn, Ridsdale Branch Rd, near Jaliparambu Junction, T0484-221 5064, www.vintageresorts.in. Wonderful, homely guesthouse with a cheerful owner. Airy modern rooms with huge baths in a quiet corner of town. Excellent value. Recommended.

Ernakulam *p62, map p68*
$$$$ Taj Gateway, Marine Dr, T0484-667 3300, www.thegatewayhotels.com. Immaculate rooms with commanding views over bay. Good restaurants, gym, bar, all business facilities and friendly service.

$$$ Abad Plaza, MG Rd, T0484-238 1122, www.abadhotels.com. A veteran of many monsoons, with large but slightly moth-eaten rooms all with a/c, fridge and cable TV. Rooms on street side can be noisy, quieter rooms on 5th floor. Breakfast included. Restaurants, gym, Ayurveda clinic, rooftop pool.

$$ Metropolitan, Chavara Rd, near Junction Station, T0484-237 6931, www.metropolitan cochin.com. Bright, spotlessly clean modern a/c rooms, excellent restaurants and service, superb value. "Best railway station hotel in South India". Recommended.

$$-$ Bharat, Gandhi Sq, Durbar Hall Rd, T0484-235 3501, www.bharathotel.com. Popular business hotel. Clean spacious rooms, some a/c, best sea-facing. Restaurant with excellent lunch *thalis* (South and North Indian). Great service, good value.

$$-$ Dwaraka, MG Rd, T0484-238 3236, dwaraka_hotel@rediffmail.com. Centrally located, family-run hotel. Good-sized, rather noisy rooms with TV, some with balcony. Only moderately clean. Adequate.

$$-$ YMCA International House, Chittoor Rd, 100 m from Central Bus Station, T0484-235 3479, www.ymcaernakulam.org. Simple rooms (some a/c), restaurant, welcoming.

$ Maple Regency, Cannon Shed Rd, T0484-235 5156. Large clean rooms, all with TV, in a great location right beside the boat jetty.

$ Modern Guest House, Market Rd, T0848-235 2130. Busy, clean hotel with helpful staff. Well-maintained rooms with bath.

$ Piazza Residency, Kalathiparambu Rd, near south railway station, T0484-237 6408. Slightly dank and musty rooms in quiet location. Good-value singles. Friendly staff.

Fort Kochi *p62, maps p64 and p66*
For a really fresh seafood meal, buy your own fish from the fishmonger stalls along the shorefront and take it to one of the nearby 'you buy, we cook' stalls, such as **Marina** or **Fort View**, where they'll be grilled or masala-fried with chips.
$$$ Malabar House Residency, (see Where to stay), Parade Rd. Excellent seafood platter and chef's salad, the latter of huge dimensions. Authentic Mediterranean and local dishes.
$$ Caza Maria (opposite hotel, see Where to stay), Jew Town Rd. 1200-2130. 2 large rooms with wooden chairs, frescoes and old framed prints on the wall. Small menu includes fish *moilee* and lime rice, *palak paneer* and *chapatti* and apple pie and ice cream. Great atmosphere.
$$ Feast, Peter Celli St. 1700-2100. With a menu focused on Keralite specialities, lovely staff that are passionate about their food and an ambient dining room, this place is a great for trying out authentic local dishes.
$ Dal Roti, 1/293 Lilly St, T0484-221 7655. Firmly established favourite for pukka North Indian food – delicious *khati* rolls, huge stuffed *parathas* – served up by the affable Ramesh and his family. Don't arrive starving as queues often stretch out the door.
$ Kashi, Burgher St, Kochi, T0484-221 5769, www.kashiartgallery.com. If you've been away a while, **Kashi** is the type of place you'll fall on in wonder. The first 2 rooms are the art gallery, the rest is a restaurant where you can drink coffee fresh from your own cafetière, or indulge in a perfect cappuccino. There's a handful of excellently made sweets and 1-2 dishes they make for breakfast or lunch.
$ Kayikka's, Rahmathulla Hotel, Kayees, New Rd, near Aanavaadal, Fort Kochi, T0484-222 6080, kayees@sify.com. 1200-1430, 1830-2030. This family concern is the busiest biryani restaurant in Kochi and a local institution. Great mutton and chicken biryanis all week with fish biryanis on Fri and prawn on Tue. Arrive early to avoid disappointment.
$ Seagull, Calvathy Rd. Good value (Rs 80 buffet lunch), pleasant veranda for drinks and dining overlooking harbour.
$ Teapot Café, Peter Celli St, T0484-221 8035, tpleaz@hotmail.com. Bare terracotta roof tiles dangle with teapots and fans, tables are tea crates and walls are hung with antique tea-related paraphernalia. Stop in for a brew of Darjeeling, Assam, Nilgiris or mint-flavoured teas, an iced coffee, or milkshake. There's a delicious selection of cakes and desserts, tasty toasted sandwiches and more substantial meals like prawn *moilee*, and mustard fish. With loads of newspapers and magazines left out for customers to read, it's a lovely place to while away a couple of hours.

Ernakulam *p62, maps p62 and p68*
$$ Bimbi's Southern Star, Shanmugam Rd. Generous portions of tasty Indian food.
$$ Khyber, Durbar Hall Rd. North Indian meals upstairs.
$$ Sealord's, Shanmugam Rd. Rooftop setting with good fish and Chinese dishes.
$$ Sri Krishna Inn, Warriom Rd, next to Chinmaya Vidya Peeth, T0484-236 6664. One of the best pure-veg places in a city of seafood, with great North and South Indian options.
$$ Subhiksha, Bharat Hotel, Durbar Hall Rd. Excellent value buffet lunch.
$ Bharat, Willingdon Island. Very good vegetarian *thalis* and Indian specialities in clean surroundings.
$ Chinese Garden, Warriom Rd. Good variety of decent Chinese meals. Alcohol available.
$ Indian Coffee House, Cannon Shed Rd. Tasty North and South Indian dishes.
$ New Colombo, Canon Shed Rd. Good snacks, fruit juices.

Cafés
Bimbi's, Durbar Hall Rd. Good fast food.
Caravan, Broadway (south). For ice creams and shakes.
Chariot, Convent Rd. Good café-style meals.
Coffee Beanz, Shanmugan Rd. Daily 0900-2300. Cold coffees, *appam*, *dosa*, popular, poky a/c coffee bar with just 6 tables.
Oven, Shanmugham Rd. Good pizzas and snacks (savoury and sweet).

⊕ Entertainment

Fort Kochi and Ernakulam *p62, maps p64, p66 and p68*
There are daily *Kathakali* performances. Arrive early to watch the extraordinary make-up being applied.
Cochin Cultural Centre, Manikath Rd, off Ravipuram Rd, Ernakulam, T0484-235 7153. A/c 'theatre', authentic performance with English explanations; 1830-1930, make-up 1730, Rs 125.
ENS Kalari, Nettoor, Fort Kochi, T0484-280 9810. *Kalarippayattu* performances, 0400-0700 and 1700-2000.
Kerala Kathakali Centre, River Rd, Fort Kochi, T0484-222 1827. Rustic surroundings but lively performance, enjoyable; 1830-1930 (make-up 1700) but check timing, Rs 100.
See India Foundation, Kalathil Parampil Lane (enter Chittoor Rd south) near Junction station, Ernakulam, T0484-236 9471. Dr Devan's 'interpreted' taste of *Kathakali* with esoteric English commentary; 1845-2000 (make-up from 1800), Rs 125.

⊕ Festivals

Fort Kochi and Ernakulam *p62, maps p64, p66 and p68*
Jan/Feb Ulsavam at the Siva Temple in Ernakulam for 8 days and at Tripunithura Temple in **Nov/Dec**. Elephant processions each day, folk dance and music performances.
Aug/Sep Onam.

⊙ Shopping

Fort Kochi and Ernakulam *p62, maps p64, p66 and p68*
Coir products (eg mats), carvings on rosewood and buffalo horn and antiques may catch your eye here. Several narrow streets in **Jew Town**, towards the synagogue, have become popular for 'antique' hunters in the last 25 years. All these shops sport a similar range of old (some faux) and new curios.
    There are several government emporia on MG Rd, Ernakulam, including **National Textiles** (another in Banerji Rd). Other shopping areas are in Broadway, Super Bazar, Anand Bazar, Prince St and New Rd.
Cinnamon, Stuba Hall, 1/658 Ridsdale Rd, Parade Ground, Fort Kochi, T0484-221 7124. Posh clothing, fabrics and interiors shop.
Dhamdhere, Pandithan Temple Rd, Mattanchery, T0484-222 4481. Interesting perfume manufacturers who confess many are synthetic (Rs 12), but the sandalwood oil is the real McCoy (Rs 100).
Idiom Books, branches on VI/183 Synagogue Lane, Jew Town and Bastion Rd, Fort Kochi, T0484-221 7075. Very good range on India, travel, fiction, religion, philosophy, etc.
Indian Industries, Princess St, Fort Kochi, T0484-221 6448. One of Fort Kochi's oldest antique dealers. Lovely family-run store with fixed prices and no-hassle browsing.

⊙ What to do

Fort Kochi and Ernakulam *p62, maps p64, p66 and p68*
Body and soul
Be Beautiful, Princess St, Fort Kochi, T0484-221 5398. Open 0900-2030. Good, cheap beauty salon with massage, hairdressers, pedicure and manicure in new premises.
Sanathana School of Yoga Studies, XV/2188-D Beach Rd Junction, T0484-229 4155, www.sanathanayoga.com. Daily classes 0730-0930 and 1630-1830, *pranayama* and *asanas* plus 28-day teacher

training programmes in a pretty residence in downtown Fort Kochi.

Tour operators

Hi! Tours, Jomer Arcade, South Junction, Chittoor Road, Ernakulam, T0484-237 7415. Efficient and well-connected inbound travel agent, who can hook you up with homestays, authentic Ayurveda retreats and responsible tour operators throughout Kerala. Helpful and highly recommended.
KTDC, Shanmugham Rd, Ernakulam, T0484-235 3234. Full- and half-day backwater tours on *kettuvallams*. Full-day tour 0830-1830 (includes lunch), half-day tour 0830-1300 and 1400-1830. Tours include visits to coir factory, spice garden, canoe ride and toddy tapping demonstration. Also daily half-day Kochi sightseeing boat cruises, 0900-1230 and 1400-1730, which cover Bolgatty Island, Chinese fishing nets, St Francis Church and Mattancherry Palace. Tour departs from Sealord Jetty.

Malabar Escapes, Malabar House (see Where to stay), 1/268-1/1269 Parade Rd, Fort Kochi, T0484-221 6666, www.malabarhouse.com.
Olympus, south end of MG Rd, Ernakulam, T0484-236 9544. Very competent and helpful.
Pepper Tours, House No 127, Subash Chandra Bose Rd, Jawahar Nagar, Kadavanthara, PO Cochin 682020, T0484-405 8886, www.peppertours.com. Memorable journeys in Kerala, Rajasthan and Goa.
Pioneer Personalized Holidays, Pioneer House, 5th Cross, Willingdon Island, T0484-266 6148, www.pioneertravels.com. Fleet of cars with tailor-made tour packages from a well-established and highly competent tour company. Efficient and knowledgeable, with unusual homestay and guesthouse options.
Sundale Vacations, 39/5955 Atlantis Junction, MG Rd, Ernakulam, T0484-235 9127, www.sundale.com. Surface and

hotel arrangements in Kerala, specializes in homestays catering to 'foreign independent tourists', promoting insight into Kerala's customs. Programmes from US$467.
Tourist Desk, Main Boat Jetty, Ernakulam, T0484-237 1761, www.touristdesk.in. One of the best budget tour operators. Daily backwater tours, 0800-1700, Rs 550, using both *kettuvalloms* and canoe. Tour includes visits to see coir making, spice garden, local village and lunch. Also 2- to 3-day tours to Wayanad and Kannur. Highly recommended.
Viceregal Travels and Resorts, S17/18 GCDA Shopping Complex, Marine Dr, Ernakulam, T0484-237 2644, www.viceregal travels.com. Runs a 9-day homestay package to charming properties, including a/c Ambassador cab, from Kochi to Peermade, Cherthala for the backwaters and Kovalam for Kanniyakumari. Rs 21,000 per person.
Visit India North Janatha Rd, T0484-233 9045, www.visitindiatravel.com. Half-day backwater tours in a dugout, punted and engineless, through very peaceful shady waterways passing unspoilt villages with toddy tappers, coir making, fishing, etc; led by an excellent guide. Rs 450 for 4 hrs, depart 0830, 1430. Highly recommended. Also offers trips in traditional *kettuvallams*; Rs 5000 (for couple) or Rs 8000 (2 bedroom); for 24 hrs, includes all meals.

⊖ Transport

Fort Kochi and Ernakulam *p62, maps p64, p66 and p68*
Air New international airport, 36 km northeast, T0484-261 0115. Prepaid taxis to Ernakulam Rs 600-800. A/c buses leave from outside the International Terminal for Fort Kochi (Rs 80) via Vytilla Junction (Rs 60), 3 km west of Ernakulam centre.

Daily domestic flights to: **Bengaluru**, **Chennai**, **Mumbai**, **Delhi** via **Goa**, **Thiruvananthapuram**; and several flights per week to **Coimbatore**, **Hyderabad**, **Kozhikode** and **Tiruchirapalli**.

International flights to: **Doha** (Qatar), **Dubai**, **Kuala Lumpur**, **Kuwait**, **Muscat** (Oman), **Sharjah** (UAE) and **Singapore**.
Airline offices All are on MG Rd unless stated otherwise. **Air India**, Durbar Hall Rd, T0484-235 1260, airport T0484-261 0070. **Emirates**, opposite Wyte Fort Hotel, NH47, T0484-337 7337. **Etihad**, Swapnil Enclave, High Court Junction, Marine Drive, T1800-223901. **Go Air**, Airport, T0484-261 0697. **Jet Airways**, BAB Chambers, Atlantis Junction, T0484-235 9212, airport T0484-261 0037. **Singapore Airlines**, c/o Aviation Travels, T0484-236 7911. **Spice Jet**, Airport, T0484-261 1750. **Sri Lankan Airlines**, T0484-236 1666.

Bus Local: Buses journey between Ernakulam, Willingdon and Fort Kochi frequently during the day. There are no local buses after 2100.
Long distance: Buses run from the KSRTC Bus Station, Chavara Rd, T0484-237 2033. There are frequent services to **Alappuzha**, every 20 mins (1½ hrs); **Kottayam**, every 30 mins (1½ hrs); **Kozhikode**, every 30 mins (5 hrs) and **Thiruvananthapuram**, every 30 mins (5 hrs). There are 7 departures daily to **Kumily** (6 hrs) or take a bus to Kottayam and change there. There is an 0630 departure to **Munnar** (4 hrs), and departures to **Kannur** at 1445 and 2345 (7 hrs). Interstate services include: 9 daily to **Bengaluru** (14 hrs) via **Kozhikode** (5 hrs) and **Mysore** (10 hrs); **Kanniyakumari**, at 1430 (7½ hrs); and **Chennai** at 1400 (15 hrs) via **Coimbatore** (5 hrs).

Private operators from **Kalloor** and **Ernakulam South bus stands** including **Indira Travels**, DH Rd, T0484-236 0693; **SB Travels**, String Dew Bldg, Tripunithura, T0484-277 7949; and **Princy Tours**, opposite Sealord Hotel, T0484-237 3109. Overnight coaches to **Bengaluru** (12 hrs) and **Mysore** (10 hrs). Departures every 30 mins to **Kottayam** (2 hrs), and **Munnar**, (4 hrs). Also to **Chennai** and **Coimbatore**.

Ferry Regular ferry services connect Ernakulam with Fort Kochi and are the fastest and easiest form of transport. Ferry tickets cost Rs 2.50. Most ferries take bikes and motorbikes. It's also possible to hire a motor boat for up to 20, from Sea Lord jetty in Ernakulam through the **KTDC** office.

Ernakulam Main Boat Jetty, Cannon Shed Rd. Ferries depart approximately every 30 mins to Fort Kochi 'Customs' jetty 0555-2130. There are also regular ferries to the Fort Kochi Mattancherry jetty (last departure to Mattencherry is 1845), and to Willingdon Island's 'Embarkation' Jetty from here. Ferries to Bolghatty depart from the High Court Jetty off Shanmugham Rd approximately every 20 mins Mon-Sat 0600-2100.

Fort Kochi The main 'Customs' jetty links Fort Kochi with Ernakulam with regular departures between 0620-2150. The last ferry leaves for Ernakulam from the Mattencherry jetty at 1930. From the northern Vypeen Jetty there are services every 30 mins to Vypeen Island between 0600-2130.

Willingdon Island There are 2 jetties: 'Embarkation' (north) and 'Terminus' (west). Ferries run every 30 mins to Ernakulam from 'Embarkation' from 0600-2110. From the 'Terminus' jetty there are irregular services to Mattencherry on Fort Kochi.

Rickshaw Auto-rickshaw drivers have a reasonably good reputation here. But, if you are likely to arrive late at night, insist on being taken directly to your hotel. A rickshaw between Fort Kochi and Ernakulam should cost around Rs 120. Fares within Fort Kochi or Ernakulam: Rs 20-40.

Taxi Ernakulam Junction to Fort Kochi, Rs 170. To airport, Rs 350-400. On MG Rd, Ernakulam: **Corp Taxi Stand**, T0484-236 1444.

Train Ernakulam/Kochi is on the broad gauge line joining Thiruvananthapuram to Mangalore, Bengaluru and Chennai.

Most trains from major cities stop at Ernakulam Junction (the main station, booking code: ERS) although a few stop at Ernakulam Town (ERN), T0484-239 0920. Enquiries: Ernakulam Junction, T131 or T0484-237 5131.

Bengaluru: *Bangalore Intercity Exp 12678*, 0910 (from ERS), 11 hrs; *Island Exp 16525*, 1755 (from ERN), 13 hrs; both via Thrissur, Palakkad and Coimbatore. **Chennai**: *Chennai Mail 12624*, 1915 (from ERN), 12 hrs. **Mangalore**: *Parasuram Exp 16650*, 1110 (from ERN), 9½ hrs); *Malabar Exp 16629*, 2350 (ERN), 10 hrs; both via Thrissur, Kozhikode and Kannur. **Thiruvananthapuram**: more than 20 trains a day, all via Kollam and Varkala.

Fort Kochi and Ernakulam *p62, maps p64, p66 and p68*

Banks In Ernakulam most banks congregate on MG Rd, including **ING Bank** and **Federal Bank**, and on Shanmugham Rd, including **State Bank of India**. All have ATM's. Most banks open till 1500. There are also several banks with ATMs in Fort Kochi including **ICICI** and **Federal Bank**, both on Chelaikada Rd. **Thomas Cook**, Palal Towers, 1st floor, MG Rd, T0484-236 8164 (Mon-Sat 0930-1800), changes TCs and currency. In Fort Kochi there are several foreign exchange offices on Princess St and Bastion St. **Medical services** General Hospital, Hospital Rd, Ernakulam, T0484-238 1768. **Govt Hospital**, Fort Kochi, T0484-222 4444. On MG Rd: **City**, T0484-236 1809, and **Medical Trust Hospital**, T0484-235 8001, have 24-hr pharmacies. **City Dental Clinic**, T0484-236 8164. **Useful contacts** Tourist Police: T0484-266 6076, help with information of all kinds. **Visa extension**: City Police Commissioner, High Court Ferry Station, Ernakulam, T0484-236 0700. **Foreigners' Regional Registration Office**, T0484-235 2454.

Munnar and Idukki's high ranges

Inland from the plains around Kottayam and Kochi lie the foothills of the Western Ghats, swathed in tropical evergreen forests and an ever-creeping tide of monoculture rubber plantations. As you climb higher these give way to pepper and cardamom, until finally you reach the rolling tea plantations and rarefied air of landlocked Idukki District. To the south sits Thekkady and the unmissable Periyar National Park, home to tiger, wild elephant, and an innovative project that is steadily turning yesterday's poachers into tomorrow's tour guides. Overnight treks into the park's hinterland offer an unmatched opportunity to see big animals up close and on foot, but even on a day visit Periyar can show you some impressive nature: wild boar foraging along the lakeside, butterflies as big as bats bouncing beneath the canopies of prehistoric jack trees, and the thud-thwack-holler as unruly gangs of Nilgiri Langur swoop through the high branches of giant figs.

Munnar, meanwhile, five hours uphill from Kochi, is *chai* central: a surreal rippling mosaic of yellow-green tea bushes and red dust roads stretching from valley deep to mountain high, with dark granite peaks pointing like fingers toward the bald grassy dome of South India's highest mountain, Anaimudi. At 1600 m, Munnar is much higher than Thekkady and gets genuinely cold, a fact that made it a favourite summer bolthole for the raj. Wildlife tourists flock to the nearby Eravikulam National Park for a glimpse of the endangered but semi-tame Nilgiri thar, a variety of ibex, while further to the north are the forests and deeply etched ravines of magnificent, rarely visited Chinnar Wildlife Sanctuary.

Arriving in Munnar and Idukki's high ranges

Getting there and around

The nearest transport hub for Munnar is Kochi-Ernakulam; Thekkady (Periyar Reserve/ Kumily town) is best accessed from Kottayam. There are no train links to the high ranges; buses take a minimum of four hours to climb the hills to both hill stations, and roads linking the two take the same length of time. ▶▶ *See Transport, page 88.*

Tourist information

District tourism offices are at **Kumily** ⓘ *T0486-922 2620*, and **Old Munnar** ⓘ *T04865-253 1516.*

The Midlands (Kottayam to Thekkady) → *For listings, see pages 84-89.*

An interesting drive to the hills, this route follows the Ghat road, which has superb views down the east side of the Ghats onto the Tamil Nadu plains. You may meet herds of Zebu cattle, buffalo and donkeys being driven from Tamil Nadu to market in Kerala. Above 1000 m the air freshens and it can be cold. Be prepared for a rapid change in temperature.

Pala, off the Kottayam–Thekkady road, is a town famous for its learned citizens – graduates of the European-style Gothic university, which was built, along with the Gothic church, by one of its affluent sons. Nehru visited in the 1950s and said that Pala was full of "people of vision". The town was the most literate place in India long before Kerala achieved 100% literacy, and Meenachil Taluka has the highest proportion of educated women in the country. It is also famous for its tamarind and pepper as well as the rubber estates belonging to the Dominic family, who serve hot Syrian-Catholic lunches in their 100-year-old plantation bungalow and 50-year-old estate mansion. Plantation tours to watch latex collection and packing can be arranged through **CGH Earth**, see page 60.

Further east lies **Erattupetta**, whose grey St George's Church holds naïve wood-painted doves and disembodied cherubims, and which hosts the **High Range Festival** every April. Carry on for **Vagamon**, a village set on a chain of three hills: Thangal, Murugal and Kurisumala. A dairy farm here is managed by Kurisumala monks.

Some 25 km south from Vagamon is **Peermade**, named after Peer Mohammed, a Sufi saint and crony of the royal family of Travancore. It is surrounded by tea, rubber and cardamom plantations, including **Abraham's Spice Garden**, where a member of the family gives excellent spice tours for Rs 50. Buses between Kottayam and Kumily can drop you here.

Many Hindu pilgrims make the journey to the forest shrine dedicated to Sri Aiyappan at **Sabarimala**, 191 km north of Thiruvananthapuram (see box, page 79). Aiyappan is a particularly favoured deity in Kerala and there are growing numbers of devotees. The shrine is only open on specific occasions: **Mandalam**, mid-November to the end of December; **Makaravilakku**, mid-January; **Vishu**, mid-April; **Prathistha** one day in May-June; and during the **Onam** festival in August-September.

Thekkady (Periyar National Park, Kumily Town) → *For listings, see pages 84-89.*

Covering 930 sq km of montane forest and grassland and centred on an attractive lake, the **Periyar National Park**, 115 km east of Kottayam, may not throw up many tiger sightings nowadays, but still attracts more than 300,000 visitors a year for its beautiful setting and unique range of soft adventure activities. Elephants, *gaur* and wild boar, though by no means guaranteed, are regularly spotted from the lake cruise boats, while sloth bear, porcupine and Malabar giant squirrel also haunt the woods.

The sanctuary was established by the old Travancore State government in 1934 and brought under the umbrella of Project Tiger in 1973, but Periyar's finest hour came in 1998 when the Kerala Forest Department, in partnership with the World Bank and the Thekkady Wildlife Society (a local NGO), set up a project to deploy a band of reformed cinnamon poachers from the surrounding villages as tour leaders and forest rangers in remote parts of the park. The camo-clad members of the **Ex-Vayana Bark Collectors Eco Development Committee** now earn a steady income from tourism, not to mention new-found respect within their communities, and their hard-won knowledge of the terrain and sharp instincts for animal behaviour makes them skilled, if not exactly chatty, forest guides. Trekking with them for a day represents your best chance of getting up close with elephants.

The centre of activities in the park is the boat jetty on pretty **Lake Periyar**, 3 km down a beautiful forest road from the tourist village of **Kumily**, which was created in 1895 by a dam that inundated 55 sq km of rich forest. A 180-m-long tunnel now leads the water eastward into the Suruli and Vaigai rivers, irrigating extensive areas of Ramanathapuram and Madurai districts in Tamil Nadu.

Hidden away in the hills to the south is **Sabarimala**, the focus of what some say is the world's biggest annual pilgrimage: 55 million pilgrims a year, almost all men, trek through

Periyar National Park

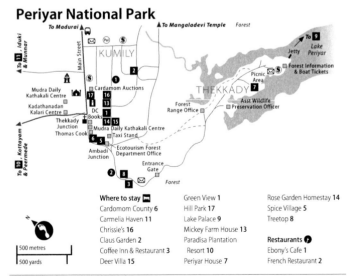

Where to stay 🛏
Cardomom County **6**
Carmelia Haven **11**
Chrissie's **16**
Claus Garden **2**
Coffee Inn & Restaurant **3**
Deer Villa **15**

Green View **1**
Hill Park **17**
Lake Palace **9**
Mickey Farm House **13**
Paradisa Plantation Resort **10**
Periyar House **7**

Rose Garden Homestay **14**
Spice Village **5**
Treetop **8**

Restaurants 🍴
Ebony's Cafe **1**
French Restaurant **2**

A modern mass pilgrimage

Sabarimala pilgrims are readily visible in many parts of South India as they wear black *dhotis* as a symbol of the penance they must undergo for 41 days before they make the pilgrimage. In addition to the black dress, pilgrims must take two baths daily and only eat food at home during this period. The pilgrimage, which begins at Deepavali, is only for males and prepubescent and post-menstrual females, to avoid the defilement believed to be associated with menstruation.

The pilgrimage in January is deliberately hard, writes Vaidyanathan, because "the pilgrimage to the shrine symbolizes the struggle of the individual soul in its onward journey to the abode of bliss and beatitude. The path of the spiritual aspirant is always long, arduous and hazardous. And so is the pilgrimage to Sabarimala, what with the observance of severe austerities and trekking up forested mountains, risking attacks from wild animals".

the forest to the shrine, which is where the god Ayyappan is believed to have meditated after slaying a demoness.

Arriving in Thekkady (Periyar National Park, Kumily Town)

Getting there and around With the exception of a couple of government-run hotels down by the lakeside, everything that happens in Periyar happens in the busy little tourist trap of Kumily. The bus stand is at the north end of the main street, a 10-minute walk from most hotels. Buses run down to the lake jetty, or you can hire a bike (a tough ride back up the hill without gears), take an autorickshaw, share a jeep, or take the pleasant walk through the woods. ▸▸ *See Transport, page 88.*

Tourist information Entry to the park costs Rs 300 per day, Rs 150 for children; Indians pay Rs 25/Rs 5. The best time to visit is December to April, when dry weather brings animals closer to the lake. Dawn and dusk are best for wildlife, so stay overnight (winter nights can get quite cold). Avoid weekends and holidays, and especially the **Makaravilakku** festival in mid-January, which brings pilgrims by their millions to the Sabarimala shrine (see box, above). **Eco Tourism Office** ① *Ambady Junction, Kumily, T0486-922 4571, www.periyartigerreserve. org*, has information and books tickets for all treks and tours in the park. **District Tourism Information Office** ① *T0486-922 2620*, runs plantation tours to Abraham's Spice Garden (4 km) and Vandiperiyar (18 km).

Activities

The standard way to see Periyar is to take a trip across the lake on a **motor launch** ① *depart 0730, 0930, 1115, 1345 and 1530, Rs 150; tickets on sale 90 mins before departure, no advance reservation required*. You can get good wildlife sightings on the first trip of the morning – elephants, gaur, wild boar, sambar and Barking deer are regularly spotted browsing on the banks, and packs of dhole (wild dog) very occasionally seen. However, noisy boats (and their occupants) and the heat soon drive animals away from the shore. Jeeps begin queueing at the park entrance gate from 0500 to get on the first launch of the morning, and there's a mad sprint to the ticket office once you reach the lake's edge.

From the same office you can book a three-hour **forest trek** ① *maximum 5 people, depart 0700, 0730, 1000, 1030, 1400, 1430, Rs 300, no advance reservations so get to office early to queue; carry water and beware of leeches*. There are good chances of seeing Malabar giant squirrel and Nilgiri langur, but much depends on your guide and not everybody comes face to face with a herd of elephants; some return very disappointed. Guides may also offer to arrange unofficial private walking tours in the park periphery in the afternoon (not the best time for spotting wildlife); try to assess the guide before signing up.

A more rewarding option is to sign up for one of the longer adventures into the park offered by the **Ex-Vayana Bark Collectors Eco Development Committee**. If you only have a day to spend in the park, spend it on the **bamboo rafting trip** ① *Rs 2000*, a full-day odyssey on land and water, trekking through a mosaic of grasslands, dense forest and rocky lakeshore, and navigating a long stretch of the lake on rickety rafts. Bird sightings are fabulous, with Malabar giant hornbill a real possibility, and the ex-poacher guides have been known to change the route to pursue – in a strictly non-violent sense – herds of elephant. A rifleman accompanies every group to ward off the threat of a charge.

If you've got longer, the **Tiger Trail** covers much the same ground but offers a chance to trek deeper into the forest, camping out for one or two nights (Rs 5000/7000 per person, maximum of six guests). Other activities include the **Jungle Patrol** (an exciting three-hour night trek, where you might spotlight porcupine and nightjars); the full-day **Border Hiking Trail** to a peak overlooking the Kambam Valley; and **bullock cart rides** to a traditional farming village.

Around Thekkady
There are a number of attractions within easy reach of Thekkady. These include the traditional Keralite-style **Mangaladevi Temple**, set amongst dense woodland on the peak of a 1337 m hill, 15 km northeast of Thekkady. Permission to visit the area must be obtained from the Wildlife Warden in Thekkady, though the temple itself is only open during the **Chithra Pounami** holiday. Other picturesque spots around Thekkady include **Pandikuzhi** (5 km) and **Chellarkovil** (15 km).

Munnar → *For listings, see pages 84-89. Phone code: 04865. Altitude: 1520 m.*

A major centre of Kerala's tea industry, Munnar sits in the lee of Anaimudi, South India's highest peak at 2695 m, and is the nearest Kerala comes to a genuine hill station. The landscape is European Alpine, minus the snow, plus tea bushes – inestimable millions of them. The town is surrounded by about 30 tea estates, among them the highest in the world at Kolukkumalai, yet despite the increasingly commercial use of the hills you can still find forests that are rich in wildlife, including the endangered Nilgiri tahr. The workers on the tea estates are mostly Tamilians who moved here eight or nine generations ago. The surrounding hills are also home to the rare Neelakurunji orchid (*Strobilanthes*), which covers the hills in colour for a month once every 12 years (next due 2018). During the monsoon cotton wool swabs of cloud shift and eddy across hillsides sodden as a sponge with fresh rains, and springs burst their banks and surge across the pathways where villagers, dark-skinned tribals in ski jackets and woollen noddy hats, swing past on Enfields on their way home from a day on the tea plantations.

Munnar

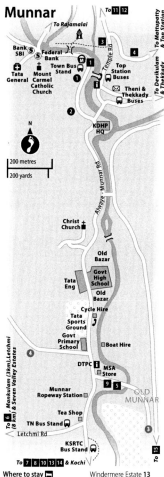

Arriving in Munnar

Getting there and around The easiest access is by bus or taxi from Kochi. There are also daily buses to Kumily and major towns in Kerala and Tamil Nadu. The town is small and pleasant for exploring on foot, although there are autos. It is worth hiring a bike or a jeep for trips out of town. ▸▸ See Transport, page 88.

Tourist information DTPC ⓘ T04865-231516, www.munnar.com, runs tours of plantations and rents cycles. Try also the free **Tourist Information Service** in the Main Bazar opposite the bus stop, run by Joseph Iype, a veritable mine of information. For trekking information, Senthil Kumar of local eco-guiding outfit **Kestrel Adventures** (see page 88) is hard to beat .

Places in Munnar

Tata Tea Museum ⓘ Nullatanni Estate, T04865-230561, www.keralatourism.org, open 1000-1600, Rs 50, has a heap of artefacts, curios and photographs to help conjure something of the lives of the men who opened up the High Ranges to tea. The crop has grown here for over a century so relics include a rudimentary tea roller from 1905 and a wheel from the Kundale Valley Light Railway that used to transport men and materials between Munnar and Top Station. The museum has descriptions of the fully automated technology of today from the tea factory at Madupatty. The museum can also arrange a visit to this factory, watching tea pickers at work and processing.

In the centre of Old Munnar, set on a hill immediately above the road in the centre of town, is **Christ Church**. Built to serve tea estate managers and workers of the High Ranges, the last English-language service was held in 1981; it is now shared between protestant Tamil and Malayalam worshippers. The exterior is un-pre possessing: rather squat and now blackened by weathering, but inside it is a charming small church, and still contains its original

14 rows of wooden pews. Ask to see the diminutive record of births and deaths of the town's founders, the British planters. Immediately behind the church a zigzag path up the hill leads to the small pioneer cemetery that was established long before the church itself as the chosen burial ground of Mrs Eleanor Knight, General Manager Knight's 24-year-old bride who caught cholera after arriving in the High Range in 1894.

Mount Carmel Roman Catholic Church, the first Catholic church in the High Ranges, is in Old Munnar on the road up to the Tata General Hospital. The first chapel on the site was founded in 1898 by Friar Alphonse who arrived in Munnar from Spain in 1854. The present church was built by the then Bishop of Vijayapuram in 1938.

High Range Club ① *T04865-230253*, is a private members' club more relaxed than the famously 'Snooty' Ooty Club. A tradition allowed members to hang their hats on the wall of the bar after 30 years of belonging to the club – the last was hung in 1989 to make 51 hats in all. Saturday is strictly jacket and tie only and backpackers will need to scrub up well to get in any day of the week. "We like scholars and researchers, professionals and club people," says the club secretary, "they know how to move in a club." It's a wonderful place with teak floors, squash courts, library and fascinating planters to chat to if you're interested in the planters' social history.

Around Munnar

There are some excellent **cycle rides** around Munnar, not all of them steep. One ride goes up a gentle slope through a beautiful valley 8 km to the **Letchmi Estate**. There is a *chai* stall at the estate and the road continues to the head of the valley for views down to the forest. A second ride (or walk) leaves Munnar by the south road for 3 km, turning left at the Head Works Dam, then takes a right turn past Copper Castle, then left to a tea stall, viewpoint, tea and cardamom plantations, again with superb views. Continue to the next tea pickers' village for a tea stall. A shorter option for this route is to cross the dam and turn left, taking the quiet road north to the **High Range Club** and Munnar.

Mattupetty Lake ① *13 km from Munnar, T04865-230389, visits between 0900-1100, 1400-1530, Rs 5*, at an altitude of 1700 m, is flanked by steep hills and woods. It was created by the small hydroelectricity dam. To its south is the Kerala Livestock Development Board's research and cattle breeding centre, formerly the Indo-Swiss dairy project. In a beautiful semi-Alpine setting surrounded for much of the year by lush green fields, the centre offers interesting insights into the practical realities and achievements of cattle breeding in India today.

Top Station, 34 km from Munnar on the Tamil Nadu border, at an altitude of 2100 m, has some of the highest tea estates in India. It is an idyllic spot, with superb views over the Tamil Nadu plains and the edge of the Western Ghats. Stalls serve tea and soft drinks. Top Station took its name from a ropeway that connected it via Middle Station to Lower Station at the valley bottom. The small town of **Bodinayakkanur**, which can be reached on the Devikulam road, lies in the valley. Buses leave from the shelter north of Munnar post office at 0715, 0915 and 1115 bound for Kovilor, passing Mattupetty Lake and Kundala Dam. Get off at Top Station, return bus after about one hour.

Across the valley from Top Station, and around 40 km east of Munnar, the small plantation of **Kolukkumalai** officially claims to pick the highest tea leaves in the world. The drive to the ridgetop at 2175 m takes two hours (the last section on a plantation road so bad it might be quicker to get out and walk) but the effort is repaid by astonishing views across misty valleys and distant peaks. It's worth being here for sunrise; set off by 0400 and wrap up warm for the journey. A path through the tea bushes leads down to the 1930s factory, where you can sample the local product and watch the antique processing equipment in action. As the plantation is privately owned you need to join a tour to get in; **Kestrel Adventures** (see What to do, page 88) is the main operator.

Eravikulam/Rajamalai National Park ① *21 km northeast of Munnar, www. eravikulam. org, closed Feb-Mar and during the monsoons, Rs 200, camera Rs 25, video Rs 200,* was set up in 1978 to preserve the endangered Nilgiri tahr (*Nilgiri ibex*). The conservation programme has resulted in the park now supporting the largest population of the species in the world, of nearly 2000. The sure-footed wild goats live in herds on the steep black rocky slopes of the Anaimudi mountains. They are brownish, have short, flat horns with the male carrying a thick mane, and can be easily seen around the park entrance. There are also elephants, sambars, gaurs, macaques and the occasional leopard and tiger. The scenery is magnificent, though the walks into the forest are steep and strenuous. There is an easier paved path from the park entrance following the road immediately below the bare granite outcrop of the Naikundi Hill to the Rajamalai Gap. The Forest Department issues a limited number of permits to trek through the park on the **Goldsbury Track**.

Adjoining Eravikulam to the north, and spreading down the eastern slope of the ghats into Tamil Nadu, the rarely visited **Chinnar Wildlife Sanctuary** ① *contact the Forest Information Office in Munnar, T04865-231587,* offers near-guaranteed sightings of elephant and bison, and has treehouses and log huts to stay in.

The road to Kochi

The route from Kochi to Munnar is one of South India's most attractive ghat roads. The one sight of note is the is the 25-sq-km **Salim Ali Bird Sanctuary** ① *Thattekad, 70 km east of Kochi on a side road heading north out of Kothamangalam; contact Assistant Wildlife Warden, Thattekad, T0485-258 8302.* A tropical evergreen and semi-evergreen forest with teak and rosewood plantations, the sanctuary is surrounded by the Periyar River, which remains shallow most of the year. It attracts water birds and the indigenous Malabar grey hornbill, rose and blue-winged parakeet, egret, heron and mynah, while rarer birds like the Ceylon frog-mouth and rose-billed rollers are also sometimes seen here.

For hotel and restaurant price codes and other relevant information, see pages 14-17.

🛏 Where to stay

The Midlands (Kottayam to Thekkady) *p77*

$$$$ Kottukapally Nazarani Tharavad, Palai, T04822-212438, www.nazaranitharavad.com. An opportunity to stay with the Kottukapally family (Kerala political royalty). There are grand Byzantine icons, Persian carpets and Travancore brass lamps. The roomy 250-year-old Kerala/Dutch/Spanish-style house of teak, rosewood and Basel tiles has 3 roomy doubles. Book in advance.

$$$$ Serenity Kanam, at Kanam Estate, 25 km east of Kottayam off Kumily Rd, T0481-245 6353, www.malabarhouse.com. This wonderful villa hotel has just 6 huge rooms, decorated with quality art and sculpture, set in a gently restored 1920s bungalow surrounded by rubber plantations and spice gardens. There's a big pool, spa and excellent food, and you can spend a morning exploring the quiet lanes from the back of Lakshmi, the estate elephant. Far from any sights, but it's worth building in an extra night or 2 just to stay here.

$$$ The Pimenta, Haritha Farms, The Pimenta, Kadalikad Post, T0485-226 0216, www.harithafarms.com. An eco-tourism concern in a pepper-growing region. Guest numbers are limited to minimize impact on the village. 4 newly built simple cottages close to the family farmhouse. The family are advocates of the return to traditional methods of agriculture, Haritha grows bio-organic spices, medicinal herbs and tropical fruit and re-plants crops lost to monoculture tea and rubber plantations. All meals included.

$$$ Vanilla County, Mavady Estate, Teekoy, Vagamon, T0482-228 1225, www.vanillacounty.in. At the source of the Meenachil River. A charming, family-friendly place with 3 rooms within 60-year-old estate house that you share with your hosts. Coffee is from the plantation around you and you can swim in nearby natural ponds. Internet access. Price includes all meals.

Thekkady *p78, map p78*

Check www.thekkady.com for information.

$$$$ Cardomom County, Thekkady Rd, T0486-922 4501, www.cardamomcounty.com. Spacious, comfortable cottages, good restaurant, nice pool, friendly (request off-season discount). Recommended.

$$$$ Lake Palace, Lake Periyar, T0486-922 3887, www.lakepalacethekkady.com. 6 rooms in interesting building inside the reserve. Idyllic island setting with superb views and wildlife spotting. Access by free ferry (20 mins) from jetty (last trip 1600). Relaxed and informal.

$$$$ Paradisa Plantation Retreat, Murinjapuzha, Kottayam–Kumily Rd, T0469-270 1311, www.paradisaretreat.com. 10 traditionally built new cottages with beautiful antique granite pillars and room furnishings, on an organic plantation estate with stunning valley views and a pool. Yoga recommended but booking essential.

$$$$ Spice Village (CGH Earth), Thekkady–Kumily Rd, T0486-922 2314, www.cghearth.com. Cottages with elephant grass thatch (cool and dark with wide eaves), spice garden, badminton, tennis, good pool, yoga centre. Excellent restaurant, lunch and dinner buffets (Rs 500), chilled beer. Good cookery demonstrations, great Ayurvedic massage and forest walks to see smaller wildlife. Luxurious, quiet, restful, friendly, with superb service. Discounts Apr-Sep.

$$$$-$$$ Carmelia Haven, Vandanmedu (20 km north on Puliyanmala Rd), on a tea, spice and coconut plantation, T0486-827 0272, www.carmeliahaven.com. Exclusive and private, with a tree house 6 m above ground, a cave house 3 m below, and a few discreetly spaced cottages in a local style using lots of thatch. An excellent open-air restaurant serves delicious Malabari food. Tours of tea factory, cardamom plantations, treks and boating. Tea and cardamom for sale.

$$$$-$$$ Hotel Treetop, Thekkady Rd, T0486-922 3286, www.hoteltreetop.com. Clean and efficient resort of gabled cottages with all mod cons and private balconies, just on the fringes of the Periyar National Park. Family bungalow has a kitchen and living area. Library, restaurant, Ayurveda massages available.

$$$-$$ Chrissie's, Thekkady Bypass Rd, T0486-922 4155, www.chrissies.in. Modern minimalist rooms all with balcony. Lush, peaceful garden with shady seating areas to relax in. Restaurant, yoga studio.

$$$-$$ Periyar House (KTDC), 5 mins' walk from the lake, T0486-222 2026, www. periyarhousethekkady.com. Pleasant, clean and comfortable rooms. Buffet meals and strong Goan beer available. Good service.

$$-$ Claus Garden, Rosapukandam, 10 mins' uphill from bus stand behind PO, 3rd turn right, T0486-922 2320, claus. hoppe@web.de. Spacious rooms in a peaceful house surrounded by jungle. Funky communal area, book exchange, friendly chilled-out vibe.

$ Coffee Inn, Thekkady Rd, 5-mins' walk from entrance gate, T0486-922 2763, coffeeinn@satyam.net.in. Wide variety of rooms, cheaper huts in quiet garden annex 100 m down the road. Popular budget traveller hang-out. Restaurant, book exchange, friendly. No reservations – rooms are allocated on a first come first served basis.

$ Deer Villa, Thekkady Rd, T0486-922 3568, www.deervilla.com. Friendly family home boasting clean, airy rooms with balcony, fan and hot water. Breakfast included. Internet café downstairs.

$ Green View, Hotel Ambadi Junction, Thekkady Bypass Rd, T0486-922 4617, www.sureshgreenview.com. Suresh and Sulekha run a welcoming 'home away from home' in a rambling house surrounded by mango trees. Hammocks are slung out in the garden. All 16 spotlessly clean rooms have large bathrooms (towels, loo roll and soap provided). Standard and deluxe rooms have cable TV and balcony. Suresh is an ex-tour guide and can provide maps for mountain treks and walks in the area. Meals available on request, cookery classes, breakfast included. Friendly and helpful. Recommended.

$ Hill Park, Main St, T0486-268 5509, hillpark@aol.in. 17 moderately clean and basic rooms all with bath and fan. Friendly staff.

$ Mickey Farm House, Thekkady Bypass Rd, T0486-922 3196, www. mickeyhomestay.com. Pleasant airy rooms in pretty garden, all with balcony. Cheaper rooms with outside bath. Mickey runs 4- to 7-day treks to Kottayam/ Alappuzha (advance notice required). Friendly family, excellent value Recommended.

$ Rose Garden Homestay, Hotel Ambadi Junction, Thekkady Bypass Rd, T0486-922 3146, rosegardenhomestay@yahoo. co.in. Sathi has 6 simply furnished rooms, all with TV, in the back garden of her flowered house. Lots of hanging wicker chairs on porches, Lovely family provide traditional Keralite breakfasts and suppers. Discounts for long stays.

Munnar *p80, map p81*
Hotel prices throughout Munnar are high for what you get, particularly in the summer high season. Cheaper places can be found around the bazar and bus stand, where touts will greet you brandishing the cards of 25-room concrete block 'cottages'.

$$$$ Tall Trees, Bison Valley Rd (3 km south of town), T04865-230641, www.ttr. in. A drastic price hike means the rather musty cottages here offer dubious value, but the location, beneath a canopy of ancient rainforest, is undeniably magic.

$$$$-$$$ Windermere Estate, Pothamedu, T04865-230512, www.windermeremunnar.com. Standalone cottages and an alpine farmhouse with 5 rooms and an elegant and utterly comfortable planters' bungalow with 3 rooms. The whole complex is set around an enormous granite boulder, that offers sweeping views of cloud-draped mountains, and there's a fantastically light and airy reading room done out with rustic timber furniture and vaulted ceilings. Pricey but recommended.

$$$ Nature Zone, Pullipara, 5 km up dirt track off Letchmi Rd, west of TN Bus Stand, bookings on T0484-649 3301, www.thenaturezone.org. Arriving here is like stepping into Jurassic Park – you have to get out of the car and unhook the elephant-repelling electric fence. A leading outward-bound training centre with stunning valley views, the drawcards here are the jungly remoteness and the 2 rustic-chic treehouses, with branches growing right through the room. The safari tents down at ground level are OK but get pretty musty. On-site canteen serves good food.

$$$ Olive Brook, Bison Valley Rd, Pothamedu, 3 km south of Munnar, T04865-230588, www.olivebrookmunnar.com. 5 well-appointed double rooms in beautiful lush location on a cardamom farm, excellent alfresco barbecues on request. Price includes meals, trekking and cookery classes.

$$$ Tea County (KTDC), 1 km north of town, T04865-230460, www.ktdc.com. 43 immaculately kept rooms set in 3 ha of neat garden, good facilities, beautiful views, great walking, own transport essential.

$$$ The Tea Sanctuary, KDHP House, T04865-230141, www.theteasanctuary.com. 6 quaint old-fashioned bungalows on the working Kanan Devan tea estate, pukka colonial-style atmosphere plus activities like mountain biking, trekking, horse riding, golf and angling, and everything clubbable at the High Range and Kundale clubs.

$$$-$$ Royal Retreat, 500 m south of KSRTC Bus Stand, T04865-230240, www.royalretreat.co.in. Agreeable standard doubles with TV and hot water, plus excellent newly renovated garden rooms and suites with fluffy quilts and DVD players.

$$ East End, Temple Rd, T04865-230452. 18 pleasant rooms and some cottages (solar heated water), good but pricey restaurant, attractively designed, quiet garden location.

$$ John's Cottage, MSA Rd, near Munnar Supply Association, T04865-231823. Small bungalow home in a well-tended lawn running down to the river, with 8 clean rooms. Indian/Chinese food or use of kitchen.

$$ Isaac's Residency, Top Station Rd, T04865-230501. Excellent quality, 32 lovely rooms with contemporary furnishings, Executive rooms with great views, 2 restaurants, bar. Recommended.

$ Arafa Tourist Home, Upper Bazar, T04865-230302. 14 rooms with TV, phone in riverside lodge, handy for late-night bus arrivals. Noise travels, but the rooms are clean and good value.

$ Sisiram Cottage Homestay, IX/18A MSA Rd, T04865-231908, www.sisiram.com. 2-storey cottage on the riverbank, with large, nicely furnished rooms upstairs and a 3-bed apartment (**$$$**) downstairs.

$ Theresian Cottages, north of town before Tea County, T04865-230351. 3 rooms open off the shared living room of this sweet little 1930s house, and though sizes vary, each has a fireplace, chaise longue and clean bathroom.

$ Zeena Cottages, near Hill View Hotel in Tata tea plantation, T04865-230560, www.hillviewhotel.com. Basic and slightly gloomy rooms in a colonial house, but the owners are friendly and the plantation views spectacular. Ask at the Tourist Information Service in the bazar (see page 81).

The road to Kochi p83

$$$ Periyar River Lodge, Anakkayam, Kothamanagalam, T0485-258 8315, www.periyarriverlodge.com. 2-bedroom cottage in a rubber plantation on the banks of Periyar River right next to Thattekad Bird

Sanctuary. Bamboo rafting, fishing, forest treks, jeep safaris to 30-m-high waterfalls for swimming, boat and bike tours. Lounge, en suite, river views. Keralite food.

$$$ Plantation Homestay, Mundackal Estate, Pindimana, Kothamangalam Junction, T0485-257 0717, www.mundackalhomestay. com. 3 rooms in a homestay that lies deep inside a rubber, pepper and coconut plantations. Daisy is a mean cook and offers lessons (US$20), while George arranges boat trips to the bird sanctuary.

Restaurants

Thekkady *p78, map p78*
$$$ Spice Village, Thekkady Rd (see Where to stay). International, excellent food and service, rustic decor, fresh garden vegetables and chef's cooking show nightly.
$$ Coffee Inn, Thekkady Rd (see Where to stay). 0700-2200. International dishes served at tables outside under the palms, bonfire in the evening, relaxed and peaceful. Friendly but very slow service.
$ Ebony's Café, Thekkady Bypass Rd. Rooftop restaurant with huge range of Indian and international dishes.
$ Edassery's Farm Yard, NH 49 Chattupara Adimali Idukki, T04864-224210. 0600-2200. Makes a good break on the Kottayam– Kumily road with tasty soups and meals, *dosa* and vegetable stews.
$ French Restaurant , Thekkady Rd. Good bread, muesli, snacks and coffee.
$ Our Place, next to Jungle View Homestay, Rosappukandam. Run by a British-Indian couple, this cozy café serves comfort food from back home alongside excellent Indian vegetarian options.

Munnar *p80, map p81*
$$ The Greens, East End (see Where to stay). Pleasant, glassed-in veranda serving good food, or go for the cheap simple meals in the eatery below.

$$ Royal Retreat (see Where to stay). International. Very pleasant, wide choice.
$ Saravana Bhavan, MG Rd. Clean, cheap and friendly place serving great *dosas* and huge Kerala-style *thalis* on banana leaves.
$ Silver Spoon, near Munnar Inn. For good breakfast choices.

Bars and clubs

Munnar *p80, map p81*
High Range Club, T04865-230253. Charming colonial-style planters' club, members only (or with reciprocal arrangements), visit by asking a planter to introduce you.
KDH Club, on side road opposite DTPC office. For Tata staff, old-world, visit with permission, excellent pool table.

Entertainment

Thekkady *p78, map p78*
Kadathanadan Kalari Centre, Thekkady Rd, Kumily, T0486-922 2988, www.thekkady tours.in. 1-hr demonstration of Kerala's traditional martial art, *Kalarippayattu*. Show time 1800, Rs 200, video charge Rs 250.
Mudra Daily Kathakali Centre, Thekkady Rd, Kumily, T(0)9447-157636, www.mudra Kathakali.com. Classical dance theatre show by performers from Kalamandalam school of dance. Make-up 1600 and 1830, show times 1630 and 1900. Rs125, video charge Rs 200.

Shopping

Munnar *p80, map p81*
Good for tea, cardamom and pepper.
Munnar Supply Assoc (MSA), next to tourist information. Established 1900, a bit of the old world, where you can get everything. Tailors in the bazar can copy your garments in 24 hrs. The newer Main Bazar is to the north.

Uravu, near Ambady Junction, Idukki, T(0)9387-469369, www.uravu.org. Fair trade outfit supporting local producers of agrihorticultural products, bamboo products, processed foods, handicrafts, forest honey, spices tea and coffee.

⏱ What to do

Thekkady *p78, map p78*
Eco Tourism Information Centre, Hotel Ambadi Junction, Thekkady Bypass Rd, Kumily, T0486-922 4571, www.periyartigerreserve.com. Organizes a full range of tours within the park: bamboo rafting, tiger trails with 1 or 2 nights' camping, evening jungle patrols, border hiking and treks to tribal settlements.
Forest Information Centre, near boat jetty, Thekkady. Cruise times: 0730, 0930, 1115, 1345 and 1530 (Rs 150). Nature trek: 0700, 0730, 1000, 1030, 1400, 1430 (Rs 300). No advance bookings, arrive early and queue at office.

Munnar *p80, map p81*
DTPC, Old Munnar Bazar. Runs tours to: Tea Valley, 1000-1800, Rs 250; Sandal Valley and Wildlife, 0900-1900, Rs 300.
Kestrel Adventures, PB No 44, KTDC Rd, T(0)9447-031040, www.kestreladventures.com. Senthil Kumar leads a team of 9 specialist guides, some expert in birds, others in tea growing and history. Highly recommended for camping and trekking, wildlife spotting in Chinnar Wildlife Sanctuary, and the only company in town that can get you into Kolukkumalai for sunrise. Also offers rock climbing, mountain bike tours/hire and jeep safaris.

⊖ Transport

Thekkady *p78, map p78*
Beware of 3-wheelers and guides at the bus station, who are working on commission from guesthouses. Nearly all hotels in Kumily are within a 10-min walk of the bus station.

Bus Local: Minibuses hourly from Kumily go down to **Aranya Nivas** on the lakeside, Rs 2. At Kumily jeep drivers will tell you there is no bus to Thekkady and charge Rs 50 for the trip; autos charge Rs 25 plus.
Long distance: From Kumily: frequent services to **Kottayam**, every 20 mins from 0600 (4½ hrs). Regular buses to **Kochi/ Ernakulam**, 6 per day, 1st at 0600 (6½ hrs); **Alappuzha**, 6 per day, 1st at 0600 (6 hrs); **Thiruvananthapuram**, 3 per day, 1st at 0830 (8 hrs); **Munnar**, 5 per day, 1st at 0600 (4½ hrs). Daily bus to **Kodaikkanal** (cancelled occasionally), 0630 (5½ hrs), or go to **Vathalakundu** and change. Buses also go from Thekkady itself (behind *Aranya Nivas*): frequent departures to **Madurai**, every 20 mins, from 0600 (4 hrs).

Munnar *p80, map p81*
Bike hire From tourist information office, Rs 50 per day. **Kestrel Adventures** (see What to do) has 18-speed mountain bikes.

Bus State buses start and terminate at 2 separate stands south of town, but also call at the **Town Bus Stand** near the market. Enquiries, T04865-230201. Frequent services to **Mattupetty** (30 mins), **Devikulam** (30 mins), **Adimali** (1 hr) and **Top Station** (1 hr). Daily to **Coimbatore** (6 hrs); **Ernakulam/ Kochi** (4½ hrs); **Kodaikkanal** 0700 via Udumalpettai, change for Palani and Kodai. If the Palani–Kodai Rd is closed a further bus goes to Vatalakundu and then Kodai; **Kottayam** (5 hrs); **Madurai** via **Theni** (5 hrs); **Thekkady** (4½ hrs), leaves from stop next to the post office; **Thiruvananthapuram** (9 hrs), **Thrissur** via **Perumbavoor** (5 hrs).

Jeeps/taxis Shared jeeps and minibus taxis for **Eravikulam** and **Mattupetty Lake** wait around the post office.

ⓘ Directory

Thekkady *p78, map p78*
Banks Federal Bank, Thekkady Junction, State Bank of India, Main St. Both have ATM. Thomas Cook, Thekkady Rd. **Medical services** Kumily Central Hospital, open 0900-1300 and 1630-2000, 24-hr call out for emergencies. **Post** Main St, next to bus station.

Munnar *p80, map p81*
Banks State Bank of Travancore ATM, in the centre near KDHP headquarters. **Federal Bank**, near Tata Hospital Rd, very helpful; State Bank of India, 1000-1400, Sat 1000-1200. **Medical services** Excellent Tata General Hospital, T04865-230270, on the north edge of town on the Rajamalai Rd. **Post** New Town centre.

Thrissur, Palakkad and the River Nila

The blue thread of the River Nila, Kerala's equivalent of the Ganges and the crucible of much of the state's rich cultural heritage, stitches together a collection of fascinating sights and experiences in the rarely explored central belt of Kerala between Kochi and Kozhikode. Busy Thrissur, the state's cultural capital, is unmissable in April and May when it holds its annual Pooram festival and millions pack into the city's central square, sardine-style, to watch the elephant procession and fireworks display. Coastal Guruvayur, meanwhile, is among Kerala's most sacred Hindu pilgrimage spots; it is home to one of India's wealthiest temples as well as an elephant yard where huge tuskers and their mahouts relax before they hit the road for the next festival. Inland, the Palakkad Gap cuts a broad trench through the Western Ghats, the only natural break in the mountain chain, providing a ready conduit for roads, railway lines, innumerable waves of historical migrants, and blasts of scorching air from the roasted plains of Tamil Nadu. Palakkad itself is now known as Kerala's granary, and makes a good stopover point on the route to or from Tamil Nadu.

Arriving in Thrissur, Palakkad and the River Nila

Getting there

Trains on the main north–south line stop in Thrissur and Shoranur Junction, a handy jumping-off point for the River Nila. Trains from Kerala to Coimbatore and Chennai call at Palakkad. There are bus connections from these towns to the smaller centres, though to properly explore the cultural and historical riches of the area it's much more efficient to hire a guide and driver. ▸▸ *See Transport, page 100.*

Tourist Information

Thrissur ① *Palace Rd, T0487-232 0800, www.dtpcthrissur.com.* **Guruvayur** ① *Vyjayanti Building, East Nada, Guruvayur, T0487-255 0400.* **Palakkad DTPC** ① *West Fort Rd, Palakkad, T0491-253 8996, www.dtpcpalakkad.com.*

Thrissur (Trichur) and around → *For listings, see pages 96-100. Phone code: 0487.*
Population: 317,500.

Thrissur sits at the west end of the Palakkad Gap, which runs through the low pass between the Nilgiri and the Palani hills. The route through the ghats is not scenic but it has been the most important link to the peninsula interior since Roman times. Thrissur is built round a hill on which stand the Vadakkunnathan Temple and an open green, which form the centre of the earth-shaking festivities. The town's bearings are given in cardinal directions from this raised 'Round'.

The **Vadakkunnathan Temple** ① *0400-1030, 1700-2030, non-Hindus not permitted inside except during the Pooram festival*, a predominantly Siva temple, is also known as the Rishabhadri or Thenkailasam ('Kailash of the South'). At the shrine to the Jain Tirthankara Vrishabha, worshippers offer a thread from their clothing, symbolically to cover the saint's nakedness. The shrine to Sankara Narayana has superb murals depicting stories from the *Mahabharata*. It is a classic example of the Kerala style of architecture with its special pagoda-like roof richly decorated with fine wood carving.

The temple plays a pivotal role in the **Pooram** celebrations, held during April and May. This magnificent eight-day cacophony of a festival is marked by colourful processions joined by people of all religious groups irrespective of caste. Platoons of elephants decked out in gold, palm leaves and lamps march to the Vadakkunnathan Temple carrying priests and idols, to the accompaniment of dozens of drums, cymbals and pipes. On the final day temple teams meet on the Tekkinkadu maidan for a showdown of drumming and *Kudumattam* (the name roughly translates as 'umbrella swapping' – one of Kerala's more surreal spectator sports) before a huge fireworks display brings proceedings to a close. In September and October, there are live performances of *Chakyarkothu*, a classical art form. There is a small elephant compound attached to the temple.

The **Town Hall** is a striking building housing an art gallery with murals from other parts of the state. In the **Archaeological Museum** ① *Town Hall Rd, Tue-Sun 0900-1500*, ask to see the royal chariot. Next door, the **Art Museum** has woodcarvings, sculptures, an excellent collection of traditional lamps and old jewellery. Nearby, **Thrissur Zoo** ① *Tue-Sun 1000-1700, small fee*, is known for its snake collection. The impressive **Lourdes Church** has an interesting underground shrine.

As one of the holiest sites in Kerala, Guruvayur, 29 km west of Trichur, is a heaving pilgrimage centre, filled with stalls and thronged from 0300 to 2200 with people wanting to take *darshan* of Guruvayurappan.

Some 4 km outside the town, the 16th-century **Sri Krishna Temple** is one of the richest in India, and there is a waiting list for the auspicious duty of lighting its oil lamps that stretches to 2025. On well-augured marriage days there is a scrum in which couples are literally shunted from the podium by new pairs urgently pressing behind them in the queue, and the whole town is geared towards the wedding industry. The temple has an outer enclosure where there is a tall gold-plated flagpost and a pillar of lamps. The sanctum sanctorum is in the two-storeyed srikoil, with the image of the four-armed Krishna garlanded with pearls and marigolds. Photography of the tank is not allowed. Non-Hindus are not allowed inside and are not made to feel welcome.

The temple's inner sanctum is off limits to non-Hindus, but you can visit the **Guruvayur Devaswom Institute of Mural Painting** ① *Mon-Fri 1000-1600*, a tiny educational institute where you can meet and buy finished works from the next generation of mural painters. As with *Kathakali*, the age-old decorative arts of temple culture steadily declined during the 20th century under the weakening structure of feudalism and opposition to the caste system. When the temple lost three walls to a fire in 1970 there were hardly any artists left to carry out renovation, prompting authorities to build the school in 1989. Today the small institute runs a five-year course on a scholarship basis for just 10 students. Paintings sell for Rs 500-15,000 depending on size, canvas, wood, etc.

Punnathur Kotta Elephant Yard ① *0900-1700, bathing 0900-0930, Rs 25, take care as elephants can be dangerous, buses from Thrissur (45 mins)*, is situated within a fort 4 km out of town. Temple elephants (68 at the last count) are looked after here and wild ones are trained. There are some interesting insights into traditional animal training but this is not everyone's cup of tea. Though captive, the elephants are dedicated to Krishna and appear to be well cared for by their attendants. The elephants are donated by pious Hindus but religious virtue doesn't come cheap: the elephants cost Rs 500,000 each.

At one time **Kodungallur**, 50 km southwest of Trichur on the border of Ernakulam District, was the west coast's major port, and the capital of the Chera king Cheraman Perumal. Nearby **Kottapuram** is where St Thomas is believed to have landed in AD 52. The commemorative shrine was built in 1952. Kodungallur is also associated by tradition with the arrival of the first Muslims to reach India by sea. Malik-ibn-Dinar is reputed to have built India's first Juma Masjid, 2 km from town. Tiruvanchikulam Temple and the Portuguese fort are worth visiting. The Syrian orthodox church in **Azikode** blends early Christian architecture in Kerala with surrounding Hindu traditions. Thus the images of Peter and Paul are placed where the *dvarapalas* (doorkeepers) of Hindu temples would be found, and the portico in front of the church is for pilgrims.

North of Thrissur the road and railway cut through lush countryside of paddy fields, quiet villages and craggy red hills mantled with coconut and rubber plantations, before crossing the wide sandy bed of the Bharatapuzha River at Shoranur. Known to the people who populate its banks as Nila, this is Kerala's longest river, rising on the eastern side of the Palakkad Gap and winding lazily through 209 km to spill into the Arabian Sea at the bustling fishing port of Ponnani. Though its flow is severely depleted by irrigation dams and its bed gouged by sand miners, the importance of the river to Kerala's cultural development is hard to overstate: Ayurveda, *Kathakali* and the martial art *Kalaripayattu* were all nurtured along the banks of the Nila, not to mention the cacophonous classical music that soundtracks festive blow-outs like the Thrissur **Pooram**. Folk tradition too is vibrantly represented: elaborately adorned devotees carry colourful effigies to temple festivals, snake worshippers roam house to house performing ancient rituals to seek blessing from the serpent gods, and village musicians sing songs of the paddy field mother goddess, passed down from generation to generation.

Despite all this, the Nila thus far remains refreshingly untouched by Kerala's tourism boom, and few travellers see more of it than the glimpses afforded by the beautiful train ride between Shoranur and Kozhikode. This is in part because there's little tourist infrastructure, few genuine 'sights', and no easy way for a travellers to hook into the cultural scene. Traditional potters and brass-smiths labour in humble workshops behind unmarked houses, while performers (singers and dancers by night, coolies, plumbers and snack sellers by day) only get together for certain events. With your own transport you can search out any number of beautiful riverside temples, but unless you join one of the superb storytelling tours run by local guiding outfit **The Blue Yonder** (see page 99), Kerala Kalamandalam (see below) might be the only direct contact you have with the Nila's rich heritage.

The residential school of **Kerala Kalamandalam** ⓘ *3 km south of river, Cheruthuruthy, south of Shoranur Junction, T04884-262305, www.kalamandalam.org, Mon-Fri 0930-1300, closed public holidays and Apr-May,* is dedicated to preserving the state's unique forms of performance art. Founded in 1930, after the provincial rulers' patronage for the arts dwindled in line with their plummeting wealth and influence, the Kalamandalam spearheaded a revival of *Kathakali* dancing, along with *ottam thullal* and the all-female drama *mohiniyattam*. The school and the state tourism department run a fascinating three-hour tour of the campus, 'A Day With The Masters' (US$25), with in-depth explanations of the significance and background of the art forms, the academy and its architecture, taking you through the various open air *kalaris* (classrooms) to watch training sessions. There are all-night *Kathakali* performances on 26 January, 15 August, and 9 November. *Koodiyattam*, the oldest surviving form of Sanskrit theatre, is enshrined by UNESCO as an 'oral and intangible heritage of humanity'. Frequent private buses from Thrissur's northern bus stand (ask for Vadakkancheri Bus Stand) go straight to Kalamandalam, taking about one hour.

In the bustling port town of **Ponnani** at the mouth of the Nila, the **Ponnani Juma Masjid** ⓘ *42 km northwest of Thrissur, nearest train station 21 km away at Kuttipuram; admission to non-Muslims not assured, dress conservatively, women should wear a headscarf,* was built in the mid-15th century by the spiritual leader Zainudhin Ibn Ali Ibn Ahmed Ma'bari, who employed a Hindu carpenter to design the exterior. Ignorant of traditional Islamic architecture, the carpenter carved the elaborate teak-wood facade to resemble a

Hindu temple incorporating many intricate Hindu designs. The carpenter was killed by a fall from the roof as he finished construction and lies buried inside the mosque. The nearby fishing docks are a hive of activity, but prepare for plenty of attention from local boys.

Palakkad (Palghat) → *For listings, see pages 96-100. Phone code: 0491. Population: 130,700.*

Kerala's rice cellar, prosperous Palakkad has long been of strategic importance for its gap – the only break in the mountain ranges that otherwise block the state from Tamil Nadu and the rest of India. Whereas once this brought military incursions, today the gap bears tourist buses from Chennai and tractors for the rich agricultural fields here that few educated modern Keralites care to plough using the old bullock carts (although the tradition is kept alive through *kaalapoottu*, a series of races between yoked oxen held in mud-churned paddy fields every January). The whole of Palakkad is like a thick paddy forest, its iridescent old blue mansions, many ruined by the Land Reform Act, crumbling into paddy ponds. There are village idylls like a Constable painting. Harvest hands loll idly on pillows of straw during lunch hours, chewing ruminatively on chapattis.

The annual festival of **Chinakathoor Pooram** (late February to early March) held at the Sri Chinakathoor Bhagavathy Temple, Palappuram, features a 33-tusker procession, plus remarkable evening puppet shows. Bejewelled tuskers can also be seen at the 20-day **Nenmara-Vallangi Vela**, held at the Sri Nellikulangara Bhagavathy Temple in Kodakara (early April): an amazing festival with grander firework displays than Trichur's **Pooram** but set in fields rather than across the city.

The region is filled with old architecture of *illams* and *tharavadus* belonging to wealthy landowners making a visit worthwhile in itself – but chief among the actual sights is **Palakkad Fort**, a granite structure in Palakkad town itself, built by Haider Ali in 1766, and taken over by the British in 1790. It now has a Hanuman temple inside. Ask directions locally to the 500-year-old Jain temple of **Jainimedu** in the town's western suburbs, a 10-m-long granite temple with Jain *Thirthankaras* and *Yakshinis* built for the Jain sage Chandranathaswami. Only one Jain family is left in the region, but the area around this temple is one of the only places in Kerala where remnants of the religion have survived.

Also well worth visiting in the region are the many traditional Brahmin villages: **Kalpathy**, 10 km outside Palakkad, holds the oldest Siva temple in Malabar, dating from AD 1425 and built by Kombi Achan, then Raja of Palakkad. But the village itself, an 800-year-old settlement by a self-contained Tamil community, is full of beautiful houses with wooden shutters and metal grills and is now a World Heritage Site that gives you a glimpse of village life that has been held half-frozen in time for nearly 1000 years. The temple here is called **Kasiyil Pakuthi Kalpathy** meaning Half Banares because its situation on the river is reminiscent of the Banares temple on the Ganges. A 10-day **car festival** in November centres on this temple and features teak chariots tugged by people and pushed by elephants.

Another unique feature of Palakkad is the *Ramassery Iddli* made at the **Sarswathy tea stall** ① *daily 0500-1830, iddli Rs 1.50, chai Rs 2.50.* If you spend any time on the street in South India, your morning meal will inevitably feature many of these tasty steamed fermented rice cakes. Palakkad is home to a peculiar take on the dumpling, one that has been developed to last for days rather than having to be cooked from fresh. The four families in this poky teashop churn out 5000 *iddlis* a day. Originally settlers from somewhere near Coimbatore, in Tamil Nadu, over 100 years ago, they turned to making this variety of *iddli* when there wasn't enough weaving work to sustain their families. They started out selling them door to door, but pretty soon started to get orders for weddings.

The *iddlis* are known to have travelled as far afield as Delhi, by plane in a shipment of 300. Manufacturers have started to arrive in order to buy the secret recipe.

Nelliyampathy, 56 km from Palakkad town, is a hill station with a tiny community of planters. It is famous for its oranges, but there are also orchids, bison, elephant and butterflies in abundance. The view across the Keralite plains from Seethakundu stunning; a third of the district lies spread out under you. The area has good trekking, too.

Megalith trail: Guruvayur to Kunnamkulam
The Palakkad Gap has been one of the few relatively easy routes through the ghats for 3000 years and this area is noted for its megalithic monuments. Megalithic cultures spread from the Tamil Nadu plains down into Kerala, but developed local forms. The small villages of Eyyal, Chovvanur, Kakkad, Porkalam, Kattakampala and Kadamsseri, between Guruvayur and Kunnamkulam, have hoodstones, hatstones, dolmens, burial urns and *menhirs*.

Thrissur, Palakkad and the River Nila listings

For hotel and restaurant price codes and other relevant information, see pages 14-17.

🛏 Where to stay

Thrissur (Trichur) *p91*
Reserve ahead for **Pooram**, when prices rocket.

$$$$-$$$ Kadappuram Beach Resort, Nattika Beach, southwest of Thrissur, T0487-239 4988, www.kadappurambeachresorts. com. Self-contained complex of bungalows and cottages in traditional Kerala design, but the emphasis here is on the Ayurveda and most come for the 14-day *panchakarma*. The Ayurveda centre is functional and not luxurious, but massage and medical attention are excellent. After treatments, cross the pretty river to a huge garden of coconut trees and hammocks that separates the hotel from the sea.

$$ Surya Ayurvedics, Kaipily Rd, Arimpur, T0487-231 2240, www.ayurvedaresorts. com. 10 rooms (some a/c) in impressive old buildings, vegetarian meals, Ayurvedic treatments, yoga, exchange.

$$-$ Luciya Palace, Marar Rd, T0487-242 4731, luciyapalace@hotmail.com. 35 rooms, 15 a/c, 2 suites, Large, clean and quiet rooms, TV, garden restaurant, internet next door, good service, very pleasant hotel.

$ Bini Tourist Home, Round North, T0487-233 5703. 24 rooms, TV, shower, 10 a/c, basic but clean and spacious rooms, restaurant, bar.

$ Railway Retiring Rooms. Well looked after and very good value.

Guruvayur *p92*
$$$-$$ Krishna Inn, East Nada, T0487-255 0777, www.krishnainn.com. Glossy hotel with white marble floors and spacious. 24-hr coffee shop, vegetarian, multi-cuisine **Thulasi** restaurant.

$$-$ Mayura Residency, West Nada, T0487-255 7174, www.mayuraresidency. com. 65 good-value, well-appointed rooms in high-rise hotel with excellent views from its rooftop. 24-hr coffee shop, **Amrutham** vegetarian (continental, South or North Indian) restaurant.

$$-$ Sree Hari Guest House, Samuham Rd, West Nada, T0487-255 6837. 8 big rooms, some a/c, with hot water, draped with purple crushed velvet in guesthouse stuffed with Krishnas and 1960s-style curtains.

$ Hotel Vanamala, Kusumam South Nada, T0487-255 5213. Popular with domestic tourists, 2-star hotel, very clean rooms with big beds and TV, telephone and hot water. A/c, vegetarian restaurant (Keralite food, 0600-2300), laundry.

Along the River Nila *p93*
If you're in search of Ayurvedic healing at its most authentic and traditional, the River Nila and Palakkad regions, far inland from the pore-clogging salt air coming off the Arabian Sea, are the best places in Kerala to find it. But don't come here expecting 5-star spa masseurs who'll tiptoe around your Western foibles about comfort and bodily privacy. These treatments are administered to you in the almost-raw, on hard wooden beds amid buckets of oil – and when your treatment is over your torturer may accompany you to the shower to make sure you thoroughly degrease.

$$$$-$$$ River Retreat, Palace Rd, Cheruthuruthy, T0488-426 2244, www. riverreatreat.in. Heritage hotel and Ayurvedic resort in the former (and much-extended) home of the maharajas of Kochi. Spacious rooms have a/c, TV and modern baths, great views onto large tree-filled garden that backs onto the Nila. Period furniture adds a nice touch to the airy communal areas. Tours of the local area, restaurant, bar, pool, Wi-Fi.

$$$ Ayurveda Mana, Peringode, via Kootanadu, T0466-237 0660, www.ayurvedamana.com. Authentic Ayurveda centre set in a fascinating 600-year-old *illam*, with treatments following the traditional methods of Poomully Aram Thampuran, a renowned expert in the discipline. Quiet airy rooms (all with TV) open onto shady veranda and peaceful manicured grounds. Full range of health care treatments available and specialized therapies for arthritis, sports injuries, infertility, etc. All treatments include individually assessed diet, massage and medicine.

$$$ Maranat Mana, Old Ooty–Mysore Rd, Pandikkad (an hour's drive north of Pattambi), T0493-128 6252, www.maranatmana.com. Special homestay in a traditional *namboodhiri* (Kerala Brahmin) household. Hosts Praveen and Vidya have sensitively converted the 160-year-old guesthouse attached to their ancestral home into 3 cool and airy rooms, all with fans and modern baths. You can visit the sprawling main family residence, one of the last surviving examples of Keralite *pathinaru kettu* ('four courtyards') architecture, which contains a Ganesh shrine to which devotees flock from far and wide. Delicious vegetarian meals included, and local tours, Ayurvedic treatments, yoga classes, cultural activities can be arranged. Fascinating and highly recommended, reservations essential.

Palakkad (Palghat) *p94*

$$$$ Kalari Kovilakom, Kollengode, T0492-326 3155, www.kalarikovilakom.com. Ayurveda for purists. Far from the Ayurveda tourist traps, the Maharani of Palakkad's 1890 palace has been restored to make this very elite retreat. It's extremely disciplined yet very luxurious: the indulgence of a palace meets the austerity of an ashram. Treatments include anti-ageing, weight loss, stress management and ailment healing. Lessons include yoga, meditation, Ayurvedic

cookery. Strictly no exertion (no sunbathing or swimming). No mod cons (TV, etc), bar, internet. US$414 per day all-inclusive. Minimum stay of 14, 21 or 28 days.

$$$ Kairali Ayurvedic Health Resort, Kodumbu, T0492-322 2553, www.kairali.com. Excellent resort, beautifully landscaped grounds, own dairy and farm, pool, tennis, extensive choice of treatments (packages of Ayurveda, trekking, astrology, golf, pilgrimage), competent and helpful staff. Recommended.

$$$ Kandath Tharavad, Thenkurussi, T0492-228 4124, www.tharavad.info. A magical place tucked away in Palakkad's fields, 6 rooms in a 200-year-old mud and teak ancestral home with natural dyed floor tiles of ochre, terracotta and blue. Nadumuttams open out onto the stars and doors are thick wedges of teak and brass. Bagwaldas, your gracious host, will guide you through local customs and culture as engagingly as he steers you through the physical landscape.

$$$ Olappamanna Mana, Vellinezhi, T0466-228 5797, www.olappamannamana.com. Majestic manor house, in rosewood, teak and jackfruit trees, to the highest Keralite Hindu caste of *namboodris*, parts of which date back 3 centuries. Pure vegetarian cuisine, no alcohol, 6 bedrooms, with bathroom and fan, no a/c.

$$ Garden House (KTDC), Malampuzha, T0491-281 5217. 17 somewhat chintzy rooms in a 1-star government restaurant on hilltop overlooking the Malampuzha Dam, a popular picnic spot. Mostly non-a/c rooms, pleasant.

$$-$ Fort Palace, West Fort Rd, T0491-253 4621. 19 rooms, groovy old-style hotel some good a/c, restaurant, brash mock turrets. Satellite TV and hot water. Continental/Indian food in restaurant, and bar, both gloomy and packed (lawn service). Nice shared sit-out on 1st floor, spotless, large double beds. Chandeliers, wood panelling.

$$-$ Indraprastha, English Church Rd, T0491-253 4641, www.hotelindraprastha.com. Kitsch and cool: 30 rooms in 1960s block, dark wood, leather banquettes and bronze lettering. Dark bar permanently packed, lawn service, 24-hr vegetarian coffee shop, exchange, internet, bookshop. Multi-cuisine restaurant.

🍴 Restaurants

Thrissur (Trichur) *p91*

Most **$** hotels have good restaurants, particularly **Siddhartha Regency's Golden Fork**, on Veliyannur Rd near the station. In general, though, eating out is still somewhat frowned on by the traditional Brahmin families of Kerala, so most eating options are down-at-heel *dhabas*.

$$ City Centre, next to Priya Tourist Home. Western snacks, bakery and good supermarket.

$$ Navaratna, Naduvilal, Round West, T0487-242 1994. 1000-2300. Pure vegetarian North Indian restaurant divided into booths.

$ Elite Bharat, Chembottil Lane. Good honest Keralan and South Indian food – *dosas*, *puttu*, *thalis* – served without ceremony to huge crowds of locals.

$ Sapphire, Railway Station Rd. 0630-2200. Excellent lime green and stone eatery dishing up *thalis* and the best chicken biryanis in town.

Palakkad (Palghat) *p94*

$ Ashok Bhavan, GB Rd. Modest vegetarian South Indian snacks.

$ Hotel Noor Jehan, GB Rd, T0491-252 2717. Non-vegetarian a/c restaurant that specializes in *moplah biryani* and *pathiri*, rice chappatis.

$ KR Bakes. 0900-2300. Puffs, ice creams, *halva* plus juice bar and savoury meals after 1600.

✹ Festivals

Thrissur (Trichur) *p91*

Jan-Feb Several temple festivals involving elephants are held in the surrounding villages which can be as rewarding as **Pooram** (eg **Koorkancherry Thaippoya Mahotsavam**, or **Thaipooya Kavadiyattam**, held at Sri Maheswara Temple, Koorkancherry, 2 km from Thrissur). Also held at the end of Feb is the **Uthralikavu Pooram**, at its most colourful at the Sri Ruthura Mahakalikavu Temple, Parithipra, Vodakancherry, en route to Shornur Junction.

End Mar 7-day **Arratupuzha Festival** at the Ayappa Temple, 14 km from Thrissur. On the 5th day the deity parades with 9 decorated elephants, while on the 6th day **Pooram** is celebrated on a grand scale with 61 elephants in the temple grounds.

Apr-May The magnificent 8-day **Pooram**, a grand festival with elephants, parasols, drums and fireworks, should not be missed. Several temples in town participate but particularly the Thiruvambady and Paramekkavu. It is marked by very noisy, colourful processions, joined by people from all religious groups, irrespective of caste. The festivities are held 1300-1700 and again at night from around 2000. Elaborately bedecked elephants (each temple allowed up to 15) specially decorated with lamps and palm leaves, march to the Vadakkunnathan Temple carrying priests and deities to the accompaniment of extraordinary drumming. On the final day temple teams meet on the Tekkinkadu *maidan* for the drumming and *Kudumattam* competition; the festival terminates with a huge display of fireworks.

Aug/Sep **Kamdassamkadavu Boat Races** at *Onam*. Also performances of **Pulikali**, unique to Thrissur, when mimers dressed as tigers dance to drumbeats.

Guruvayur *p92*
Punnathur Kotta
Feb/Mar Utsavam, 10 days of festivities start with an elephant race and continue with colourful elephant processions and performances of *Krishnanattom* dances. Details from Kerala tourist offices.
Nov-Dec 5-day Ekadasi with performances of *Krishnanattom*, a forerunner of *Kathakali* – an 8-day drama cycle.

⏱ What to do

Along the River Nila *p93*
Body and soul
Arya Vaidya Sala, Kottakal town, T0483-274 2216, www.aryavaidyasala.com. One of the biggest and best Ayurvedic centres in India, with a fully equipped hospital offering 4-week *panchkarma* treatments as well as on-site medicine factory and research department.
The Blue Yonder, 23-24 Sri Guru Nivas, Bengaluru, Karnataka, T080-4115 2218, www.theblueyonder.com. Award-winning responsible travel tour operator, focused on conserving local culture and traditions. Tours are carried out in a way that allows travellers to become fully immersed in the region's way of life, and travelling here can feel like being in an episode of the Arabian Nights, as the knowledgeable guides unfold local folk tales and fables. Flexible, individual itineraries can include homestays, cultural performances, monsoon rafting in self-built bamboo-and-inner-tube rafts, backwater *thoni* (country boat) cruises, legend and heritage trails and wildlife safaris. Unique in India, and heartily recommended.

⊖ Transport

Thrissur (Trichur) *p91*
Bus There are yellow-top local buses available. For long distance, there are 3 bus stands. KSRTC, near railway station, T0487-242 1842, southwest of 'Round' including several to **Alappuzha** (3½ hrs), **Bengaluru** (10 hrs), **Coimbatore** (3 hrs), **Guruvayur** (1 hr), **Kochi** (2 hrs), **Kozhikode**, **Chennai** (13 hrs), **Palakkad**, **Thiruvananthapuram** (7 hrs). North (Priyadarshini), just north of 'Round', buses to **Cheruthuruthy**, **Ottapalam**, **Palakkad**. Sakthan Thampuran, 2 km south of 'Round', for frequent private buses to **Guruvayur**, **Kannur**, **Kozhikode**.

Train Enquiries, T0487-242 3150. All trains connecting Kochi with points north stop in Thrissur. **Ernakulam**: more than 20 trains a day; *Kannur Ernakulam Intercity Exp 16306*, 1843, 1¼ hrs. **Chennai** (MC): *Chennai Mail 12624*, 2040, 10½ hrs. **Bengaluru**: *Bangalore Intercity Exp 12678*, 1020, 9½ hrs. **Mangalore**: *Parasuram Exp 16650*, 1240, 7½ hrs (via Kozhikode, 3 hrs).

Palakkad (Palghat) *p94*
Bus KSRTC, buses run from the Municipal Bus Stand, T0491-252 7298, to **Coimbatore**, **Kozhikode**, **Mannarghat** (Silent Valley), **Pollachi**.

Train The main Junction station, T0491-255 5231, is 5 km northeast of town. Some passenger trains also stop at the more central **Town** station. **Coimbatore**: frequent trains all day, 1-1½ hrs, including *Bangalore Intercity Exp 12678*, 1145, continues to **Bengaluru** (8 hrs), and *Mangalore Chennai Exp 16108*, 1435, continues to **Chennai** (15 hrs). **Ernakulam** (Kochi): many trains, including *Ernakulam Intercity Exp 12677*, 1420, 2½ hrs; all go via Thrissur, 1-2 hrs. **Mangalore**: *Chennai Mangalore Exp 16107*, 1300, 9 hrs, via Kozhikode, 4 hrs.

ⓓ Directory

Thrissur (Trichur) *p91*
Banks ATMs are everywhere, including at the railway station. **State Bank of India**, Town Hall Rd, Round East, near Paramekkavu Temple; **State Bank of Travancore** (upstairs), opposite. **Internet** Sruthy, north of temple ring. Good connections, Rs 30 per hr. **Medical services** Amala Cancer Hospital, Amalanagar (9 km, along the Guruvayur Rd), T0487-221 1950. Recommended for medicine, surgery.

Malabar coast

The Malabar region is the unsung jewel of Kerala: the combination of the state's political administration in the south plus the pious Muslim community and orthodoxy of the Hindu population have made it more resistant to tourist development than the more easy-going Catholic-influenced stretch south from Kochi. Any cohesion between north and south Kerala is political, not cultural: Malabar was under the Madras Presidency before Independence, lumped together with the Travancore south only in 1956. The atmosphere couldn't be more different. The coastal towns of Kozhikode (formerly Calicut), Thalassery and Kannur are strongholds of the Muslim Moplah community, whose long-standing trading links with the Middle East have bred a deep cultural affinity that's reflected in the lime-green houses lining the roads and the increasing number of women seen in purdah. At the same time, Malabar is one of the best places to see Kerala's Hindu religious and cultural traditions in their proper context: *Theyyam* (the ritual temple dance that spawned *Kathakali*) and *Kalaripayattu* (the stunning martial art), are both practised here. Inland from Kozhikode, the glorious hilltop district of Wayanad experiences some of the heaviest levels of rainfall in the world, and its familiar stubble of tea plantations is interspersed with some of the most stunning and accessible rainforest in the state.

Kozhikode (Calicut) → *For listings, see pages 107-110. Phone code: 0495. Population: 436,500.*

Kozhikode is a major commercial centre for northern Kerala and the centre for Kerala's timber industry; it is also dependent on the petro-dollar, as testified by the scores of direct flights to the Gulf each day. Around 1.2 million Keralites work in the Gulf, generating revenue of about US$12 billion for Kerala. The city itself is engaged in mostly small-scale retail. Off the brash and crowded main boulevard, tiny lanes thread between high laterite walls with everything happening on the street. Remnants of the spice trade remain and the markets are great. Court Road is home to pepper, the black gold that lured Vasco, as well as copra and coconut oil. There are beautiful wooden mosques built like Hindu temples, and in nearby Beypore, where the Chaliyar river meets the Arabian Sea, you still have half a chance of watching the birth of an *uru* – the massive deep-sea hauler-sized wooden boats that have been built by Muslim Khalasi shipbuilders with few technological changes since Cheraman Perumal ordered one for a trip to Arabia in the sixth century.

Arriving in Kozhikode (Calicut)

Getting there and around Karipur airport, 25 km south, has connections with the Middle East as well as several major Indian cities. The station and main bus stand are on opposite sides of the town centre, both within easy reach of several hotels. Autos are widely available and surprisingly cheap. ▸▸ *See Transport, page 110.*

Tourist information Kerala Tourism ① *Malabar Mansion hotel, SM Rd, T0495-272 1395,* has limited information about the town. The branch at the railway station hands out brochures on North Kerala and can help with hotel bookings.

Places in Kozhikode (Calicut)

The Sunni Muslim quarter of **Kuttichera**, behind the railway station to the west of town, holds several fascinating multi-tiered wooden mosques, set around a huge green pond to which flocks of white-capped elders gather in the late afternoon. Legend has it that a ghost within the pond seizes a human sacrifice each year, releasing the body after three days. The mosques date from the 15th century and bear a puzzlingly close resemblance to Hindu temple structures. **Mishkal Masjid** is one of the oldest, and was named for the wealthy trader who built it, but also look for **Jami Masjid** and **Munchunthi Palli**. The latter has a 13th-century *vattezhuthu* (inscribed slab of stone) that proclaims the donation of the land to the mosque by a Zamorin. Women should cover their head, shoulders and limbs in this area.

Note the size of the houses around here, which are known to accommodate more than 150 family members each. The *puyappala* tradition (literally translates as 'fresh husband') means that each marrying daughter takes the husband back into her parents' home. One house is supposed to have 300 people living under the same roof: each building has an average of three kitchens. From here you can walk along Beach Road, where crumbling old buildings that were once trading centres are now being busily demolished. The beach itself is more of a town latrine than a place for swimming.

Pazhassiraja Museum ① *5 km north of the centre on East Hill, Tue-Sun 0900-1630, Rs 10,* has copies of original murals plus bronzes, old coins and models of the some of the area's megalithic monuments. Next door is the **art gallery**, with an excellent collection of paintings by Indian artists as well as wood and ivory carvings, and the **Krishna Menon Museum** ① *Mon, Wed only, 1000-1230, 1430-1700, free,* dedicated to the Keralite politician who became a leading left-wing figure in India's post-Independence Congress government.

Around Kozhikode

Kappad, 16 km north, and now the site of a poor, mainly Muslim fishing village, is where Vasco da Gama and his 170 sailors landed on 27th May 1498. There is an old plaque by the approach road to the beach commemorating the event. Although it is a pleasant spot, the sea is unsuitable for swimming since pollution from Kozhikode filters down this far and the beach itself is used as a toilet by the fishermen.

Beypore, half an hour south of Calicut, was once a significant port, but is now famous only for its boatyard, where families of Khalasis have used traditional methods to make *urus* (huge wooden vessels) for 1500 years. The wiry Khalasis craft the ships using memorized plans and ancient construction techniques, now mainly for the benefit of wealthy Arab clients who deploy them as luxury yachts or floating restaurants.

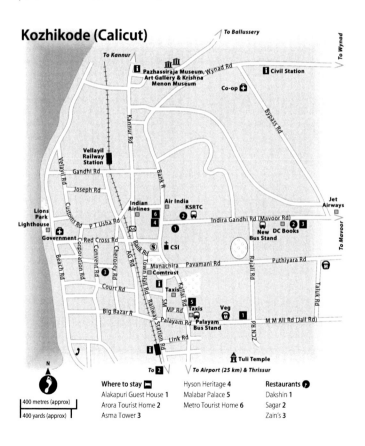

Kozhikode (Calicut)

Where to stay		Hyson Heritage 4	Restaurants
Alakapuri Guest House 1		Malabar Palace 5	Dakshin 1
Arora Tourist Home 2		Metro Tourist Home 6	Sagar 2
Asma Tower 3			Zain's 3

400 metres (approx)

400 yards (approx)

Mahé → *For listings, see pages 107-110.*

The borders of the 9 sq km that make up French Kerala are marked not by baguette bakeries or pavement cafés, but by shops screaming 'Foreign Liquor'. By night, the 35,000 residents of this outpost of Pondicherry disappear to make way for the truckers who rush through to stock up on half-price whiskies and brandies, taking advantage of the colony's special tax status. By day, however, Mahé is pretty enough: policemen wear French hats and the town is beautifully positioned on a slight hill overlooking the river. It was named after Mahé de Labourdonnais, who captured it for the French in 1725. Many people here still speak French and the very French **Church of St Theresa** celebrates its feast day on 14-15 October. The beaches to the south and north of town are dirty and are not safe for swimming due to undercurrents.

Thalassery (Tellicherry) → *For listings, see pages 107-110. Phone code: 0490.*

Like everywhere along the Malabar's increasingly gold coast, banks here have queues for gold loans where your branch manager doubles as a pawnbroker. Despite an obsession with wealth, at the wide, tree-covered street level you'll find a town that's friendly, brilliantly walkable and lined with 19th-century shops complete with original wooden cupboards and cobwebs. Author Herman Hesse's mother was born here.

Thalassery was set up by the British East India Company in 1683 to export pepper and cardamom. In 1708 they obtained permission to build a **fort** which, having survived a siege laid by Haidar Ali, is still standing today on a rocky promontory about 15 m above sea level. Its proud little gateway, raised on a flight of steps, is flanked by colourful mustachioed figures. There are some attractive old buildings. The Armenian church is rather shabby now but the Catholic church still thrives though the population is largely *Moplah* (Kerala Muslims). The **Odathil Mosque**, believed to be 400 years old, is in the traditional Kerala style with a gabled roof and copper sheeting.

Mambally's Royal Biscuit Factory ① *near the Old Police Station, T0490-232 1207, 0900-2030,* established in 1880, claims to be where cake was first baked in Kerala. Nowadays you'll find jam rolls, ketchup, Nestlé milky bars and lime pickle along with the fresh bakes. The downstairs of the double-decker shops is crowded with hessian sacks full of cinnamon from China, cloves from Madagascar, raisins from Afghanistan and star anise from China and Vietnam. Some of the owners are third generation traders.

The **fish market** ① *0600-1800,* is one of the liveliest in Kerala. Men with cleavers stand tall over barracudas and manta, while stacks of clams, mussels, shrimp and mackerel are constantly replenished with new loads. Fish are then sped along the state highway to reach markets in Kochin and Mangalore.

Thalassery is also a centre for training in gymnastics and circus acts, so street performers and acrobats are not uncommon; 90% of India's circus companies originate here. You can see martial arts in local *kalaris*: one of the best being the tricky-to-find *kalari* of **K Viswanathan Gurukkal** ① *MKG Kalari Sangham, Kuzhippangad, PO Chirakkara, T0490-237110, call in advance.*

Muzhapilangad Beach, 8 km from Thalassery, is nicknamed 'Drive In Beach'. It is an unspoilt, beautifully picturesque 4-km-long stretch of golden sand edged by palm trees at the northern end. Amazingly empty most of the time, it earned its nickname from the local custom of ragging trucks and Ambassadors up and down its firm sands.

Kannur (Cannanore) → *For listings, see pages 107-110. Phone code: 0497.*

Standing on raised ground with cliffs at the sea face, this town boasts a coconut-fringed coastline with some attractive beaches. Weavers' co-operatives and *beedi* factories provide employment but this is also a good place to watch *Theyyam* dances. DTPC ① *at the railway station, T0497-270 3121, www.dtpckannur.com.*

The centre of the Moplah community (a group of Arab descent), Kannur was also the capital of the North Kolathiri Rajas for several hundred years. **Fort St Angelo** ① *0900-1800* was built out of laterite blocks by the Portuguese in 1505 and taken over by the British in 1790 as their most important military base in the south. The picturesque **Moplah town** is round the bay to the south of the fort. The attractive **Payyambalam Beach** is 2 km away.

Handloom weavers produce silk and cotton saris, shirts, *lungis* and soft furnishings sold through local cooperatives. **Kanhirode Weavers' Cooperative Society** ① *Koodali Kannur, T0497-285 7259, 0900-1700, free,* was founded in 1952 on Gandhian principle, has a yearly turnover of Rs 150 million (US$3.7 million) and exports 95% of its pure handloom fabric to the UK for the Futon Bed Company. Spun cotton is shipped in from Coimbatore, and dyed in huge vats after which the cooperative's 450 staff are expected to feed bobbins through the high wooden looms fast enough to make 42 m within 3½ days for women, or three for men. While some weave, others feed the raw heaps of cotton from wire frames onto wheels to make thread – in the silk section they use bicycle wheels. The daily wage is Rs 100 (US$2.45), and apparently the co-op is having trouble recruiting more of the caste, who, as caste rules relax, are going for higher paid jobs elsewhere. A visit here is well worth the journey.

Bekal and Kasaragod → *For listings, see pages 107-110. Phone code: 04994.*

Bekal, 16 km south of Kasaragod, has an ancient **fort** on the sea, the largest and best preserved in Kerala, which gives superb views of the coastline. Originally built by the Kadamba kings, the fort passed under the control of Vijayanagar and of Tipu Sultan before being brought into the hands of the East India Company. Excavations have exposed some interesting structures. Just outside the fort is the **Sri Mukhyaprana Temple**. North and south of the fort stretch long, largely unspoiled beaches, whose sands the Kerala tourism authorities visualize as a future Kovalam; so far there are just a couple of outlandish and isolated resorts. En route to Bekal the road passes **Ezhimala**, with a beach and a hill famous for its Ayurvedic herbs.

Kasaragod is the northernmost town in Kerala. From the bus stand, the walk to the sea through a sprawling residential area – mainly Moplah – takes about 30 minutes. The beach is magnificent and deserted. You can walk a long way before scrambling back to the main road, crossing paddy fields, backwaters, and the Konkan railway line. For *Theyyam* and *Yakshagana* performances contact the **Kasaragod DTPC** ① *Vidya Nagar, T04994-256450, www.dtpckasaragod.com.*

Wayanad → *For listings, see pages 107-110. Phone code 04936.*

The forest-shrouded shoulders of Chembra Peak stand guard over Wayanad ('land of paddy fields'), a beguiling highland district of spice farms, tea plantations, waterfalls and weird upwellings of volcanic rock, inland from Kozhikode on the picturesque road to Mysore. An easy weekend break from either city, Wayanad so far remains delightfully unspoiled, and its cool misty mornings make a refreshing contrast with the sultry coastal plains. It's also prime wildlife spotting territory: elephants patrol the woodlands of Muthanga and Tholpetty sanctuaries, while the dense *shola* forests around Vythiri are home to whistling thrushes, leaping frogs and giant squirrels. Many of the plantation bungalows have thrown open their doors as luxurious, atmospheric homestays, and the vogue for building treehouses makes this the best place in India if you want to wake up among the branches of a fig tree looking out over virgin forest.

Arriving in Wayanad

Getting there and around The main transport hubs are Kalpetta and Sultan Bathery, with buses from both to Kozhikode and Mysore, and from Sultan Bathery south to Ooty. Local buses connect these towns to the smaller villages, with jeeps and auto-rickshaws available for local transfers. However, hiring a car can save a lot of time and hassle.

Tourist information DTPC ① *north Kalpetta, T04936-202134, www.dtpcwayanad.com*, is run by the efficient and knowledgeable Dinesh, who is a good source of information on trekking and wildlife.

Places in Wayanad

The road from Kozhikode to Wayanad corkscrews steeply up the Western Ghats, topping out after 65 km at **Vythiri**, a popular but low-key weekend getaway set amid stunning forests, with kayaking and nature walks available at **Pookot Lake**. At Chundale (5 km from Vythiri) the road divides: the main route continues to busy **Kalpetta**, which offers plenty of hotels and banks but little in the way of charm, while the more appealing Ooty road leads east to **Meppadi**, the starting point for treks up wild and rugged **Chembra Peak** (2100 m) ① *Forest Range Office, Kalpetta Rd, Meppadi, T04936-282001, trekking Rs 1000 per group including guide; call ahead to check the track is open*, on whose summit lies a heart-shaped lake. Beyond Meppadi the road continues through the rolling teascapes of Ripon Estate, then through cardamom, coffee, pepper tree and vanilla plantations to reach **Vaduvanchal** (18 km). Six kilometres south of here, **Meenmutty Falls** ① *Rs 600 per group including guide (ask for Anoop, who speaks English and knows the forest intimately)*, are Wayanad's most spectacular waterfalls, tumbling almost 300 m in three stages. An adventurous forest track leads down to a pool at the base of the second fall; take your swimming things.

Sulthan Bathery (Sultan's Battery), the main town of western Wayanad, was formerly known as Ganapathivattom, or 'the fields of Ganapathi'. In the 18th century Tipu Sultan built a fort here, but not much of it remains. Some 12 km southwest of the town are the **Edakkal Caves**, a natural deep crevice set high on a granite hill on which engravings dating back to the Neolithic era have been discovered. Around 30 km to the east is **Muthanga Wildlife Sanctuary** ① *0700-0900 and 1500-1830 (last entry 1700), Rs 100, Indians Rs 10, guide fee Rs 100 per group, jeep entry Rs 50; jeeps can be hired for Rs 300 per safari*, the least developed section of a giant reserve that also includes Karnataka's Bandipur and Tamil Nadu's Mudumalai National Parks. Jeep rides in the sanctuary, noted for its elephants, leave from the entrance gate.

Malabar coast listings

For hotel and restaurant price codes and other relevant information, see pages 14-17.

🛏 Where to stay

Kozhikode (Calicut) *p102, map p103*

$$$ Harivihar Ayurvedic Heritage Home, Bilathikulam, T0495-276 5865, www. harivihar. com. In Calicut's pretty Brahminical suburbs, this immaculate former royal home is surrounded by lawns with giant mango and jackfruit trees and a beautiful green water tank where you can undertake pukka Ayurveda or study Indian philosophy, Sanskrit, vasthu and yoga in a small guesthouse setting run by conventional medics. You can also stay on a B&B basis, in one of 5 doubles and 3 singles. Gentle Sivananda yoga, Ayurveda from Coimbatore Arya Vaidya Pharmacy, no alcohol.

$$$ Tasara, Calicut–Beypore Rd, Beypore, T0495-241 4832, www.tasaraindia.com. A weaving centre amid a garden of mango and jackfruit trees. Rooms with fan and basic bath. Vasudevan, Balakrishnan and their sisters have been running textile workshops here since 1979, and guests come to take courses in weaving, block-printing, batik, silkscreen and natural dyeing. Price includes all meals, tuition and activities. Good discounts for monthly stays, reservations essential.

$$ Hotel Asma Tower, Mavoor Rd, T0495-272 3560, www.asmatower.com. 44 a/c and non-a/c rooms in gleaming new tower. Inside, expect 2-tone mint green decor, frosty a/c system, perfumed air, muzak and TV and telephone in every room. Good value.

$$ Malabar Palace, GH Rd, Manuelsons' Junction, T0495-272 1511, www.malabar palacecalicut.com. 52 a/c rooms, excellent a/c restaurant, bar, very helpful reception.

$$-$ Hyson Heritage, 114 Bank Rd, T0495-276 6423, www.hysonheritage.com. A breezy, efficient and well-maintained business hotel, with 89 spotless, smallish rooms with phone, cable TV, bath, 47 a/c, set around a large courtyard. Ayurvedic treatments available.

$ Alakapuri Guest House, Moulana Mohammed Ali Rd, T0495-272 3451. 40 rooms set around a charming garden brimming with plants and trees and lotus pond. Simple, spacious, with old furniture, phone, tubs and TV. Dates from 1958, and easily Calicut's most characterful mid-range option. Bar 1000-2200, dining hall 0700-2200.

$ Arora Tourist Home, Railway Station Rd, T0495-230 6889. Not as ship-shape as the outside and ground floor suggest, but the huge rooms here are clean enough if you just want to dump your bags after a train ride. Street noise dies down overnight, but mosquitoes don't rest.

$ Metro Tourist Home, Mavoor Rd Junction, T0495-276 6029. 42 pleasing rooms in bustling hotel, some with TV, a bit noisy, South Indian restaurant. Gloomy with grubby paintwork but clean sheets, big mirrors and good fans.

$ Railway Retiring Rooms. Very spacious, clean, good service.

Thalassery (Tellicherry) *p104*

$$$$ Ayisha Manzil, Court Rd, T0490-234 1590, www.ayishamanzil.uniquehomestays. com. A delightful mid-19th century, colonial-style heritage home overlooking the sea. 6 huge a/c rooms with carved teak and rosewood furniture, massive baths, lots of British and Malabari memorabilia, amazing fresh seafood and cookery courses, temple pond pool, superb panoramic views, excursions.

$$-$ Hotel Pranam, AVK Nair Rd, Narangapuram, T0490-222 0634. 14 cleanish rooms with bath – 4 with a/c, a little grubby. The a/c deluxe room has an extraordinary green carpeted sitting room attached.

$ Paris Presidency, New Paris Complex, Logan's Rd, T0490-234 2666, www.paris presidency.com. 24 clean and comfortable rooms with baths, TV, phone, restaurant, wood furniture, bright white walls in busy shopping area. Multi-cuisine restaurant.

Kannur (Cannanore) p105
$$ Costa Malabari, near Adykadalaya Temple, 6 km south of town (by bus, ask to get out at Thazhe Chowwa), T0484-237 1761, www.costamalabari.com. An unpretentious guesthouse converted from a warehouse with 5 rooms off a main hall. The owners have authored a book on Kerala's festivals and have encyclopaedic knowledge of the local *Theyyam* scene. Difficult to get to and far from the centre, but there are 5 idyllic, wholly empty beaches within walking distance. Meals included.

$$-$ Mascot Beach Resort, near Baby Beach, Burnassery, 2 km from centre, T0497-270 8445, www.mascotresort.com. Good rooms in high-rise business hotel overlooking the residents-only pool, located in the quiet cantonment area (Ayurvedic centre attached).

$$-$ Royal Omars Thavakkara Kannur, very close to the railway station and colourful market area, T0497-276 9091. Spanking new, with spacious standard non-a/c doubles at bargain rates. 65 rooms, TV, credit cards.

$ Hotel Savoy, Beach Rd, T0497-276 0074. Bags of character in this super-clean, old-fashioned complex of bungalow cottages set around a lawn. A/c cottages are wonderfully spacious and cool. Bar attached.

Wayanad p105
Wayanad is Kerala's treehouse capital, and has superb homestay options, but offers relatively little joy at the budget end. Cheaper places are generally restricted to Kalpetta and Sulthan Bathery.

$$$$-$$$ Vythiri Resort, 6 km up dirt road east of highway, T04936-255366, www. vythiriresort.com. Beautiful resort hidden beside a tumbling forest stream, with a choice of cute *paadi* rooms (low beds and secluded courtyards with outdoor shower), high-ceilinged cottages, or a pair of superb new treehouses in the branches of fig trees, one of which involves being hand-winched up and down. Leisure facilities include spa, pool (swimming and 8-ball), badminton and yoga, and there's a good outdoor restaurant (buffet meals included in price) where you can watch monkeys trying to make away with the leftovers.

$$$ Aranyakam, Valathur (south of Ripon off Meppadi–Vaduvanchal Rd), T04936-280261, T(0)9388-388203, www.aranyakam. com. Atmospheric homestay in Rajesh and Nima's 70-year-old bungalow, set amid a sea of coffee bushes and avocado trees. Huge rooms in the elegant main house come with raked bare-tile ceilings and balconies, or opt for the valley-facing treehouses where you can look out for deer and sloth bear while watching sunset over Chembra Peak. Nima serves genuine home-style Kerala food in the thatched, open sided dining room.

$$$ Edakkal Hermitage, on road before Edakkal Caves, T04936-260123, www. edakkal. com. A sustainable tourism initiative with 5 comfortable cottages and a sweet, simple treehouse, built in, around and on top of a series of huge boulders. Tree frogs inhabit the bamboo-fringed pond, and the sunset views over paddy fields and mountain ranges are magic. The highlight, though, is dinner, served in a natural grotto that's lit with hundreds of candles. Price includes meals.

$$$-$$ Green Gates, TB Rd, North Kalpetta, T04936-202001, www.greengateshotel.com. Modern if slightly scuffed and musty rooms with a/c, TV and hot showers, within walking distance of Kalpetta's shops. There's a pool and Ayurvedic spa, and a helpful travel desk arranges trips to caves, wildlife sanctuaries and tribal colonies of Wayanad.

$$$-$ Haritagiri, Padmaprabha Rd, T04936-203145, www.hotelharitagiri.com. A modern building in the heart of Kalpetta just off the highway, some a/c rooms, clean and comfortable, restaurant 'reasonable', good value but rather noisy.

$$-$ Regency, on the main road in Sulthan Bathery, T04936-220512. Good range of neat and tidy rooms, better value at the cheaper end.

$ Dwaraka, on the main road in Sulthan Bathery, T04936-220512. Far from sparkling, but offers the cheapest rooms in town.

$ PPS Tourist Home, just off highway at south end of Kalpetta, T04936-203431. Reasonable rooms, good cheap restaurant.

$ YMCA Camp, off the highway in Vythiri, T(0)9895-544609. There's just one simple room in this peaceful encampment, but it's big, cool and exceptional value.

🍴 Restaurants

Kozhikode (Calicut) *p102, map p103*
$$ Malabar Palace (see Where to stay). International, a/c, excellent food and service.
$ Dakshin, 17/43 Mavoor Rd, T0495-272 2648. 0630-2230. Dead cheap place for *dosa*, pizza, cutlet and curd rice (meals from Rs 15).
$ Hotel Sagar, 5/3305 Mavoor Rd, T0495-272 5058. 0530 onwards. So popular they've launched their own hotel, and another restaurant (the original is already multistorey). **Sagar** is famous for its biriyanis, and also does superb breakfasts of *dahl* and *parotta*. Upstairs is for families and a/c rooms; downstairs is the cattle class.
$ Zain's Hotel, Convent Cross Rd, T0495-276 1482. A simple place run by a Muslim husband and wife. Mussels, biriyanis for Rs 30 and fish curries for Rs 15.

Thalassery (Tellicherry) *p104*
$$ Ayisha Manzil, Court Rd, T0490-234 1590. Peerless homestay, serving food unlike you'll get anywhere outside a home. Phone for meals in advance.
$ Royal Visitors' Family Restaurant, Pranam Tourist Home, T0490-234 4292. 0630-2300. Grilled mussels, etc.

Kannur (Cannanore) *p105*
$$ Chakara Drive in Restaurant, Cliff Exotel International, Payyabalam, T0497-271 2197. Specials are sizzlers plus spicy fried *kallumakais* mussels and Malabar biriyani.
$ Indian Coffee House, Fort Rd. For snacks.
$ Mascot Beach Resort's Restaurants, near Baby Beach, Burnasseri, T0497-270 8445, www.mascotresort.com. Some of the best top-end eating in town.
$ MVK Restaurant, SM Rd, T0497-276 7192. 1000-2200. A local institution which has been packed from its opening 50 years ago, thanks to its commitment to fresh, home-ground spice mixes for its biriyanis, their rice grains steeped in ghee. Serves beautiful, potent lime tea too.
$ Regency Snacks and Fast Food, opposite Sangeetha Theatre, SN Park Rd, T0497-276 8676. Popular café with locals.
$ Your Choice Restaurant, Fort Rd. Authentic Malabari food.

🎭 Entertainment

Kannur (Cannanore) *p105*
Theyyam dance
At **Parssinikadavu Temple**, 20 km north of Kannur, reached by bus. Performances (Dec-Mar) of ritual dance theatre at dawn (taxi essential) and often late afternoon to dusk. Pilgrims sometimes seek blessing from the principal dancer who may go into a trance after taking on the role of Mutthapan, a manifestation of Siva as Hunter.

⛳ What to do

Kannur (Cannanore) *p105*
PVA Ayurvedic Multi Speciality Nursing Home, Onden Rd, T0497-276 0609, www.pvaayurvedic.com. The down-at-heel PVA provides training courses in Ayurveda as well as rejuvenation, purification packages and direct treatments for ailments like disc prolapse, psoriasis and obesity. The 3 doctors here are highly regarded.

Bekal *p105*
Bekal Resorts Development Corporation,
T0467-227 2007, www.bekal.org. The
tourism-starved north wants a piece of the
houseboat action. Happily it has amazingly
pristine mangroves.

Wayanad *p105*
The Blue Yonder (see page 99) can
arrange excellent, forest-savvy guides.

⊖ Transport

Kozhikode (Calicut) *p102, map p103*
Air Airport, T0495-271 1314 (Domestic),
T0495-271 0517 (International). Transport
to town: prepaid taxi Rs 300. **Air India**,
Eroth Centre, Bank Rd, T0495-276 7401;
airport, T0495-271 3700, flies to **Mumbai**,
Coimbatore, **Goa**, **Chennai**, **Tiruchirapalli**.
Jet Airways, Arayedathupalam, near BM
Hospital, T0495-274 0052, to **Mumbai**.
International flights to **Abu Dhabi** (UAE),
Bahrain, **Doha** (Qatar), **Jeddah** (Saudi
Arabia), **Kuwait**, **Muscat** (Oman), **Ras-Al-
Khaimah** (UAE) and **Sharjah** (UAE).

Bus KSRTC, T0495-272 2771, from bus
stand Mavoor Rd (near Bank Rd junction)
to **Bengaluru**, **Thiruvananthapuram** (via
Thrissur, Ernakulam, Alappuzha, Kollam),
0630-2200 (10 hrs), **Ooty** (see Wayanad,
below). The **New Bus Stand**, T0495-272
2823, is further east on Mavoor Rd for private
buses to the north including **Kannur**. Local
buses operate from **Palayam Bus Stand** on
Kallai Rd, T0495-272 0397.

Train Enquiries, T0495-270 1234. Trains to
Chennai, **Coimbatore**, **Ernakulam** (4½ hrs)
via **Shoranur** and **Thrissur**, **Goa**, **Mangalore**
(5 hrs), **Mumbai**, **Thiruvananthapuram**
(9½-10 hrs).

Kannur (Cannanore) *p105*
Bus Enquiries: T0497-270 7777. To
Kozhikode (2½ hrs), **Mangalore** (4½ hrs),
Mercara (6 hrs), **Mysore** (6 hrs).

Train Enquiries: T0497-270 5555. To
Mangalore: *Chennai Mangalore Mail 12601*,
0940, 2¾ hrs; *Parasuram Exp 16650*, 1740,
2½ hrs. **Palakkad**: *Kannur Yesvantpur Exp
16528*, 1745, 5 hrs, continues to **Bengaluru**
(YPR), add 9 hrs; *Mangalore Chennai Mail
12602*, 1550, 5 hrs, continues to **Chennai**, add
10 hrs. **Ernakulam (Kochi)**: *Kannur Ernakulam
Intercity Exp 16306*, 1430, 5½ hrs.

Wayanad *p105*
Bus From Kalpetta Bus Stand, T04936-
203040, to **Kozhikode**, 3½ hrs, via **Vythiri**;
Mysore via **Sulthan Bathery**. From Sulthan
Bathery, T04936-220217, to **Ambalavayal**
(for Edakkal Caves), **Vaduvanchal** and **Ooty**.

❶ Directory

Kozhikode (Calicut) *p102, map p103*
Banks ATMs on Kallai Rd and at station.
Exchange at SBI, Bank Rd. Good rates, no
commission, friendly. Also **Thomas Cook**.
Internet Nidhi, near New Bus Stand or
behind **Malabar Mansion**, SM St. Fast, Rs 30
per hr. Sreeram Travels, shop 3, opposite
district hospital. **Medical services**
Government Hospital, T0495-236 5367.
Medical College Hospital, T0495-235 6531.

Thalassery (Tellicherry) *p104*
Banks Federal Bank, MM Rd, 1000-1530
(Sat 1000-1230 Sun closed) for speedy
transactions. **Internet** Telynet Internet
Café, Masjid Building near Municipal Office,
MG Rd, telynet@rediffmail.com. 0900-2100.

Kannur (Cannanore) *p105*
Internet Search World, near Railway
Station, MA Rd. Fast connection, Rs 30 per hr.

Wayanad *p105*
Banks ATMs in Kalpetta and Sulthan
Bathery. For exchange, try UAExchange, on
the main road in Kalpetta. **Internet** Several
places in Kalpetta and Sulthan Bathery.

Lakshadweep, Minicoy and Amindivi Islands

The islands, which make up the Lakshadweep ('100,000 islands'), have superb beaches and beautiful lagoons. There are, despite the name, only 11 inhabited and 11 uninhabited islands making up the group. Minicoy, the southernmost island, is 183 km from Kalpeni, its nearest neighbour. Geologically they are the northernmost extensions of the chain of coral islands that extends from the far south of the Maldives. The atolls are formed of belts of coral rocks almost surrounding semi-circular lagoons, with none more than 4 m above sea level. They are rich in guano, deposits of centuries of bird droppings. The wealth of coral formations (including black coral) attracts a variety of tropical fish including angel, clown, butterfly, surgeon, sweetlip, snappers and groupers. There are also manta and sting rays, harmless sharks and green and hawksbill turtles. At the right time of the year you may be able to watch turtles laying their eggs. Arriving on the beach at night, each lays 100-200 eggs in holes they make in the sand.

Arriving in Lakshadweep, Minicoy and Amindivi Islands

You can only visit the islands on a package tour – individuals may not book independently. Lakshadweep Tourism's **Society for Promotion of Recreational Tourism and Sports (SPORTS)** and other tour operators organize package tours. Everyone needs a permit, for which you need to provide details of the place and date of birth, passport number, date and place of issue, expiry date and four photos; apply two months ahead. If you plan to dive, get a doctor's certificate. Foreign tourists may only visit Bangaram and Kadmat Islands; Indians can also visit Kadmat, Kavaratti, Kalpeni and Minicoy. Thinakkara and Cheriyam are being developed. ▸▸ *See What to do and Transport, pages 113-114.*

The islands → *For listings see pages 113-114. Population: 60,600. 225-450 km west of Kerala. Total land area: 32 sq km.*

Kavaratti, the administrative capital, is in the centre of the archipelago. The Ajjara and Jamath mosques have the best woodcarvings and the former has a particularly good ceiling carved out of driftwood; a well nearby is believed to have medicinal water. The aquarium with tropical fish and corals, the lake nearby and the tombs are the other sights. The woodcarving in the Ajjara is by superb local craftsmen and masons. Kayaks and windsurfers are available for rent, there's a dive centre, plus a bank and a few *dhabas* selling local food.

Some of the other islands in this group are **Andratti**, one of the largest which was first to be converted to Islam, and **Agatti**, which has Lakshadweep's only airport, a beautiful lagoon and a palm-shaded resort.

Barren, desolate and tiny, **Pitti Island** comprises a square reef and sand bank at its south end. It is a crucially important nesting place for terns and has now been listed as a wildlife sanctuary. Conservation groups are pressing for a ban on the planting of trees and the mining of coral, but the main risk to the birds is from local fishermen who collect shells and the terns' eggs for food. Nearby **Cheriam** and **Kalpeni** have suffered most from storm damage.

Bangaram is an uninhabited island where **CGH Earth** runs the **Bangaram Island Resort** (see Where to stay, below).

Kalpeni, with its group of three smaller uninhabited satellite islands, is surrounded by a lagoon rich in corals, which offers excellent snorkelling and diving. The raised coral banks on the southeast and eastern shores are remains of a violent storm in 1847; the Moidin Mosque to the south has walls made of coral. The islands are reputedly free from crime; the women dress in wrap-around *lungis* (sarongs), wearing heavy gold ornaments here without any fear. Villagers entertain tourists with traditional dances, *Kolkali* and *Parichakkali*, illustrating themes drawn from folk and religious legends and accompanied by music and singing.

Minicoy (Maliku), the southernmost and largest island, is interesting because of its unique Maldivian character, having become a part of the archipelago more recently. Most people speak *Mahl* (similar to *Dhivehi*; the script is written right to left) and follow many of their customs. The ancient seafaring people have been sailing long distances for centuries and the consequential dominance by women may have led Marco Polo to call this a 'female island'. Each of the nine closely knit matrilineal communities lives in an *athir* (village) and is headed by a *Moopan*. The village houses are colourfully furnished with carved wooden furniture. Tuna fishing is a major activity and the island has a cannery and ice storage. The superb lagoon of the palm-fringed crescent-shaped island is enclosed by coral reefs. Good views from the top of the 50-m lighthouse built by the British. You can stay at the **Tourist Huts**.

The **Amindivi** group consists of the northern islands of **Chetlat**, **Bitra** (the smallest, heavily populated by birds, for a long time a rich source of birds' eggs), **Kiltan** where ships from Aden called en route to Colombo, **Kadmat** and the densely populated **Amini**, rich in coconut palms, which was occupied by the Portuguese. **Kadmat**, an inhabited island 9 km long and only 200 m wide, has a beach and lagoon to the east and west, ideal for swimming and diving. The **Tourist Huts** shaded by palms are away from the local village. The Water Sports Institute has experienced, qualified instructors. There are 10 executive and **Tourist Cottages** and a **Youth Hostel** with a dorm for 40.

Lakshadweep, Minicoy and Amindivi Islands listings

For hotel and restaurant price codes and other relevant information, see pages 14-17.

⬤ Where to stay

Lakshadweep, Minicoy and Amindivi Islands *p111*
Kavaratti and Kadmat have basic tourist cottages resembling local huts. Each hut has 1-2 bedrooms, mosquito nets, fans and attached baths; electricity is wind or diesel. Meals are served on the beach and are similar to Keralite cuisine, with plenty of coconut. Breakfast might be iddlis or puris with vegetables. Lunch and dinner might be rice and vegetable curry, sambhar, meat or fish curry. Vegetarian meals available on request. Alcohol is available on board ship and on Bangaram Island (tourists requested not to carry it though).

$$$$ Bangaram Island Resort,
T0484-301 1711, www.cghearth.com. 26 standard huts on the beach with fan, fridge and bathrooms or 3 deluxe beach huts which sleep 4. Activities include scuba-diving, snorkelling, deep-sea fishing and kayaking. International cuisine served.

⬤ What to do

Lakshadweep, Minicoy and Amindivi Islands *p111*
Tourism is still in its infancy and facilities on the islands are limited. Package tours (the only way to visit) are relatively expensive. Tours operate Oct-May; most are late Jan to mid-May. Schedules may change, so allow for extra days when booking onward travel.
CGH Earth, Kochi, see page 60. For the resort only, US$250-350 (for 2), US$500-700 for 4, US$70 extra person (discounts Apr-Sep). On Bangaram, kayaks, catamarans and sailing boats are free. For an extra charge each time: scuba diving (equipment for hire); deep-sea big-game fishing 1 Oct-15 May – only minimal fishing equipment and boat crew; excursion to 3 neighbouring islands or snorkelling at shipwreck (for 8); glass-bottomed boat. Snorkelling in the lagoon can be disappointing due to poor visibility and dead corals. Kadmat Island scuba-diving US$800, 1-star CMAS Certificate US$30; certified diver US$25 per dive; adult US$350, child (under 10) US$165. Travel by ship from Kochi (deck class) included; return air from Kochi or Goa to Agatti, US$300; return helicopter (Agatti-Kadmat), 15 mins, US$60, or local *pablo* boat.
SPORTS (Lakshadweep Tourism), Indira Gandhi Rd, Willingdon Island, Kochi, T0484-266 8387, T0484-266 6789. 3 packages costing Rs 6000-10,000 per person (student discounts), including transport from Kochi. **Coral Reef**: 5 days to Kavaratti, Kalpeni and Minicoy Islands. **Kadmat Water Sports**: 6 days (including 2-day sailing, stay in **Kadmat Cottages** or hostel). **Paradise Island Huts**: 6 days to Kavaratti.

Tour operators

For a full list of authorized tour operators, see www.lakshadweeptourism.com/agents.html.

Watersports

Activities include windsurfing, scuba-diving (**Poseidon Neptune School**), parasailing, waterskiing and snorkelling. Deep-sea fishing (barracuda, sailfish, yellow-fin, travelly) is possible on local boats with crew; serious anglers should bring their own equipment; no diving or deep-sea fishing Apr-Sep.

⊖ Transport

Lakshadweep, Minicoy and Amindivi Islands *p111*

Air Agatti has a basic airport. **Indian Airlines** and **Kingfisher** fly to/from **Kochi**, daily except Tue and Sun.

Ferry *MV Tipu Sultan* sails from **Kochi**. 26 passengers in 1st and executive class have 2- and 4-berth a/c cabins with washbasins, shared toilets, Rs 5000; 120 passengers in 2nd class in reclining seats in a/c halls, Rs 3500. Ship anchors 30-45 mins away from each island; passengers are ferried from there. Total travel time from Kochi can take up to 30 hrs.

Inter-island transfers are by helicopter (when available) during monsoons, 15 May-15 Sep (return US$60), or by *pablo* boats for 8.

❶ Directory

Lakshadweep, Minicoy and Amindivi Islands *p111*

Agatti has a medical centre; emergencies on the islands have helicopter back-up.

Contents

Footprint features

Background

History

The **Cheras**, who established themselves in the Kuttanad region around Alappuzha as the first Kerala power, developed a wide network of trade links in which both the long-established Christian community and the Jewish community participated fully. However, the neighbouring Cholas launched several successful attacks against Chera power from AD 985. When Chola power disintegrated at the end of the 11th century, Calicut gradually became dominant under the **Zamorin** (literally 'Lord of the Sea'), who had well-established contacts with the Arab world. By some accounts the Zamorins were the wealthiest rulers in contemporary India, but were never able to use these advantages to unite Kerala, and during the 16th century the Portuguese exploited the rivalry of the Raja of Kolattiri with the Zamorin of Calicut, being granted permission to trade from Kochi in 1499. Over the following century there was fierce competition and sometimes open warfare between the Portuguese, bent on eliminating Arab trading competition, and the Zamorin, whose prosperity depended on that Arab trade. After a century of hostility, the Dutch arrived on the west coast. The Zamorin seized the opportunity of gaining external support, and on 11 November 1614 concluded a treaty giving the Dutch full trading rights. In 1615 the British East India Company was also given the right to trade by the Zamorin. By 1633 the Dutch had captured Portuguese forts. The ruler of Kochi rapidly made friends with the Dutch, in exchange for having the new Mattancherry Palace built for him. In the decade after 1740 Raja Marthanda Varma succeeded in uniting a number of petty states around Thiruvananthapuram and led them to a crushing victory over the Dutch in the Battle of Kolachel in 1741. By 1758 the Zamorin of Calicut was forced to withdraw from Kochi, but the **Travancore** ruler's reign was brief. In 1766 Haidar Ali had led his cavalry troops down onto the western coastal plain, and he and his son Tipu Sultan pushed further and further south with a violence that is still bitterly remembered. In 1789, as Tipu was preparing to launch a final assault on the south of Travancore, the British attacked him from the east. He withdrew his army from Kerala and the Zamorin and other Kerala leaders looked to the British to take control of the forts held by Tipu's officers. Tipu Sultan's first defeat at the hands of Lord Cornwallis led to the Treaty of Seringapatam in 1792, under which Tipu surrendered all his captured territory in northern Kerala, to direct British rule. Travancore and Kochi then became Princely states under ultimate British authority.

Modern Kerala

Government Kerala politics have often been unstable – even turbulent – since the first elections were held in March 1957, when Kerala became the first state in the world to democratically elect a Communist government. In contrast to many other parts of India, politics in Kerala have remained mostly secular, as the Hindu BJP's failure to gain a substantial foothold suggests. The debate has always been dominated by the struggle between the Marxist branch of the Communist Party of India (CPI-M), the Congress and various minor parties; and the state government has often been formed by coalitions. Since the late 1970s these have formed around two relatively stable "fronts": the Congress-led United Democratic Front, and the CPI-M Left Democratic Front. Control of the state has passed back and forth between the two at every election since 1982, with the UDF holding power at the time of writing in early 2014.

Kerala's social underbelly

Although you'll get the sense of living under one long coconut palm thicket, locals have good reason to call Kerala the city state; the ratio of people per square metre outstrips that of anywhere else in India. And don't let the socialist rhetoric of their political parties fool you – in the main, Keralites are a prosperous bunch and money and status certainly matters. Kerala is where the marketing people come to test their advertising campaigns, and the state boasts of how highly it scores in all quality of life indicators. But relative affluence brings with it social problems: Kerala also has both the highest suicide rate and one of the highest rates of alcohol consumption per capita on the subcontinent, and huge swathes of agricultural land go uncultivated as high literacy creates a class with loftier ambitions than tilling the soil.

Economy Traditionally Kerala's economy has depended heavily on agriculture. Estate crops, especially tea and rubber, make a major contribution to exports, while coconut and coconut products like coir (the coarse fibre used for matting and string and rope production), or copra (the oil-rich flesh of the coconut), continue to be vital to the state. Recent decades have seen the rise of Kerala as a remittance economy, with large flows of money being repatriated by Malayali workers in the Gulf to invest in land, housing and small-scale industries. Highly educated and increasingly middle class, Keralites have been abandoning old-fashioned and 'menial' industries such as agriculture. Rice production has been in long-term decline, as farmers converted paddy land to other more profitable uses, and where farm fields still exist, they are largely run by Tamils or other migrant workers – who in turn earn more in Kerala than in their home states. However, the collapse of Dubai's building boom looks set to trigger a reverse exodus, with hundreds of thousands of workers expected to return to Kerala in the next few years. The challenge this poses to the state is enormous, not only in supporting the families affected, but in managing a population whose aspirations and debts have been built around Gulf salaries. Business leaders bemoan the leftist culture of the state and the stranglehold the trade unions have on its workforce, which makes for a working week dominated by strikes, thus barring the way for the high levels of foreign investment that characterize Bengaluru, Hyderabad and Chennai's urban economies.

Culture

The distinctiveness of Kerala's cultural identity is reflected in the Brahmin myths of its origin. As Robin Jeffrey explains, Parasurama, the sixth incarnation of Vishnu, having been banished from India, was given permission by Varuna, the Lord of the Sea, to reclaim all the land within the throw of his axe. When Parasaruma threw the axe it fell from Kanniyakumari to Gokarna, and as the sea withdrew Kerala was formed.

Matriarchy This may have originated in the 10th-century conflict with the Cholas. Krishna Chaitanya suggests that as many men were slaughtered there was a surplus of women, encouraging the development of a matrilineal system in which women controlled family property. Kerala is the first state in India to claim 100% literacy in some districts and

Body language

Ayurveda, a Sanskrit word meaning 'the knowledge (*veda*) of life (*ayur*)', is an Indian holistic system of health dating back over 5000 years. Indians see it as a divine gift from Lord Brahma, their Hindu creator God, which has been developed by sages and holy men over the centuries. In contrast to the Western system of medicine, which is geared to treating an already diseased body or mind, Ayurveda seeks to help the individual strengthen and control both mind and body in order to prolong life and prevent illness. In today's world, it's a brilliant complement to Western medicine and, as well as detoxing the body and mind and relieving stress, has been used to treat ME, high blood pressure, allergies, asthma, back pain, rheumatism, skin diseases, migraines and insomnia, and is used as an effective follow-up treatment to chemotherapy.

How it works In essence, Ayurveda combines body treatments and detoxification therapies with a balanced diet, gentle exercise and meditation to promote wellbeing. The type of treatments and therapies are dictated by an individual's constitution, defined by a balance of three bodily energies or *doshas*: *vata*, *pitta* and *kapha*. Composed of the five elements – earth, water, fire, air and ether (or space) – these *doshas* govern our bodily processes: *vata* controls circulation and the nervous system; *pitta* the metabolism and digestion; *kapha* bodily strength and energy. When we feel out of kilter, our *doshas* are likely to be out of balance, which a course of Ayurvedic treatments will seek to remedy. If we're uptight and prone to multi-task, it will calm us down and help us focus. If we're sluggish and suffer from bad digestion, it will energize us and get our bowels moving again.

An experienced Ayurvedic doctor will diagnose your *dosha* type by taking your pulse, and observing such things as how quickly you speak and move, your build, the colour of your eyes and the quality of your skin. You'll also be asked lots

women enjoy a high social status. The 2001 Census shows that overall literacy has reached 91%, and uniquely in India there are more women than men in the population.

Religion The majority of the population is Hindu, but as much as a quarter is Christian and there is also a large Muslim population. Religious communities have often lived amicably together. There is no conflict between the varying Hindu sects, and most temples have shrines to each of the major Hindu divinities. Christianity, which is thought to have been brought by St Thomas the Apostle to the coast of Kerala at Kodungallur in AD 52, has its own very long tradition. The equally large Muslim community traces its origins back to the spread of Islam across the Indian Ocean with Arab traders from the seventh century.

Cuisine Kerala's cuisine reflects its diverse religious traditions, its location on the seaboard and the ubiquitous presence of the coconut. Uniquely in India, beef is widely eaten, although seafood is far more common. Fish *moilee* is prepared with coconut milk and spices while for *pollichathu* the fish is baked with chilli paste, curry leaves and spices. Coconut-based dishes such as *thoran*, a dry dish of mixed vegetables chopped very small, herbs and curry leaves, and *avial*, similar to *thoran* but cooked in a sauce, are widely eaten.

of questions about your preferences – on anything from climate to the spiciness of food. The more open and honest you are, the more accurate a judgement will be, though it's uncanny how the best doctors will read you just right, whatever you tell them.

What you do Any programme of Ayurveda will include preparation treatments and elimination (or detox) therapies. The former include soothing, synchronized oil applications and massages, and swedana (purifying steam and herbal baths), while the latter involve ingesting or retaining herbal medicines, medicated oils and ghee (or clarified butter), inhalations, bastis (or oil enemas), therapeutic vomiting and bloodletting. Preparation treatments often include sleep-inducing shirodara, when a wonderful continuous stream of warm oil is poured across your forehead; choornaswedana, where hot herbal or lemon poultices are massaged all over you to induce sweating; and the supremely nourishing four-handed *abhyanga* and *marma* massage. *Pizhichil* is often regarded as the 'Marmite' of Ayurveda. Gallons of cleansing sesame oil are poured continuously over your body and massaged in by two therapists as the oil increases in heat. You'll slip about like a sardine in a tin, but this treatment is very effective. Look at the oil afterwards, and you'll be shocked at just how dirty you were. If you're a smoker, it's likely to be black.

Any hotel or retreat venue that offers only Ayurvedic massages is offering only a part of what Ayurveda is all about. You need time for Ayurveda treatments to have any real effect. A proper course of Ayurveda needs at least two weeks to be effective and offer any real lasting benefit, and rest between treatments is vital. Most people who undertake a course of Ayurveda have wa 'panchakarma' – which literally translates as five therapies, and which also refers to a general Ayurveda detox lasting two weeks or more.

Erisseri is a thick curry of banana or yam and *kichadi* is beetroot or cucumber in coconut-curd paste. You can try these with the soft centred, lacy pancake *appam* or the soft noodle rice cakes *iddiappam*. Jack fruit, pineapples, custard apples and an endless variety of bananas also play a vital part in many dishes. For dessert, you might get milk *payasam*, made with rice or vermicelli.

Language Malayalam, the state language, is the most recent of the Dravidian languages, developing from the 13th century with its origin in Sanskrit.

Dance The special dance form of Kerala, *Kathakali*, has its origins in the *Theyyam*, a ritual tribal dance of North Kerala, and *Kalaripayattu*, the martial arts practised by the high-caste Nayars, going back 1000 years. In its present form of dance-drama, *Kathakali* has evolved over the last 400 years. The performance is usually outdoors, the stage bare but for a large bronze oil lamp, with the drummers on one side and the singers with cymbal and gong, who act as narrators, on the other. The art of mime reaches its peak in these highly stylized performances which used to last through the night; now they often take just three to four hours. The costume is comprised of a large billowing skirt, a padded jacket, some heavy ornaments and headgear. The make-up is all-important: *Pacha* (green) characterizing the Good and *Kathi* (knife, shape of a painted 'moustache'), the Villain; *Thadi* (bearded), white for superhuman *hanumans*, black for the hunter and red for evil and fierce demons; *Kari* (black) signifying demonesses; *Minukku* (shining) 'simple' make-up representing the Gentle and Spiritual. The paints are natural pigments while the stiff 'mask' is created with rice paste and lime. The final application of a flower seed in the lower eyelid results in the red eyes you will see on stage. This classical dance requires lengthy, hard training to make the body supple, the eyes expressive. The 24 *mudras* express the nine emotions of serenity, wonder, kindness, love, valour, fear, contempt, loathing and anger. The gods and mortals play out their roles amid the chaos brought about by human ambition, but the dance ends in peace and harmony restored by the gods.

Land and environment → *Population: 32 million. Area: 39,000 sq km.*

Stretching from some of the highest mountains of the Western Ghats to the lush coastal plain, Kerala encapsulates the rich diversity of western India's coastal landscapes. Its narrow coastal fringe has been raised from the sea in the last million years. Inland are rolling hills of laterite, succeeded by the ancient rocks that form the backbone of the Western Ghats.

Contents

Footnotes

Language

Want to impress your hosts with a few words of Malayalam? Go ahead and try: the Malayalis boast that their language is one of the hardest in India to learn. In contrast to the clipped tones of Hindi, spoken Malayalam gushes forth in a torrent of words, with barely a discernable gap in between. Then there's the matter of negotiating the common, almost unpronounceable, diphthong 'zh'. Forget about Brezhnev, and put your tongue in the position of the English R, with the tip not quite touching the roof of the mouth, and then try to pronounce the Z of 'zoo'. If you make a sound that's halfway between a Z and the S of 'pleasure', you're ready to march up to the nearest banana seller and demand a bunch of *vaazha pazham*.

Malayam words and phrases

English	Malayalam
Basics	
hello, good morning, goodbye	*namaskaaram*
thank you	*nandi*
no, thank you	*venda, nandi*
excuse me, sorry	*kshamikkanam*
yes	*athe/uvvu*
no	*illa/alla*
never mind/that's all right	*kuzhappamilla*
Questions	
what is your name?	*ningalude peru enthaanu?*
my name is …	*ente peru … ennaanu*
pardon?	*enthaa?*
how are you?	*engane undu?*
I am well, thanks, and you?	*enikku sukahamaanu, nandi, ningalkko?*
not very well	*nalla sukhamilla*
where is the …?	*… evide aanu?*
who is?	*aaraanu?*
what is this?	*ithu enthaanu?*
Shopping	
how much?	*enthaanu vila?*
that makes (20) rupees	*ithinu irupathu roopayaanu*
that is very expensive	*athu valare kooduthalaanu*
make it a bit cheaper	*vila kurackanam*
The hotel	
what is the room charge?	*room charge ethra aanu?*
please show the room	*dhayavaayi room kanickaamo?*
is there an air-conditioned room?	*A C room undo?*

is there hot water?	*choodu vellam kittumo?*
… a bathroom/fan/mosquito net…	*…bathroom/fan/kothuku vala…*
is there a large room?	*valiya room undo?*
please clean it	*dhayavaayi vrithiyaakkamo*
are there clean sheets/blanket?	*vrithiyulla sheet/puthappu undo?*
bill please	*bill tharaamo?*

Travel

where's the railway station?	*railway station evide aanu?*
how much is the ticket to Agra?	*aagrayilekkulla ticket charge eth ra aanu?*
when does the Agra bus leave?	*aagrayilekkulla bus eppol purappedum?*
how much?	*ethra?*
left/right	*idathu/valathu*
go straight on	*nere pokoo*
nearby	*aduththu*
please wait here	*dhayavaayi ivide wait cheyyoo*
please come at 8	*dhayavaayi ettu manikku varoo*
quickly	*vegam*
stop	*nilkkoo*

Time and days

right now	*ippol thanne*	Monday	*thinka*
morning	*raavile*	Tuesday	*chovva*
afternoon	*uchacku*	Wednesday	*budhan*
evening	*vaikunneram*	Thursday	*vyaazham*
night	*raathri*	Friday	*velli*
tomorrow	*naale*	Saturday	*shani*
month	*maasam*	Sunday	*njaayar*
year	*varsham*		
day	*divasam*		
week	*aazhcha*		
today	*innu*		
yesterday	*innale*		

Numbers

1	*onnu*	14	*wpathinaalu*
2	*randu*	15	*pathinanchu*
3	*moonnu*	16	*pathinaaru*
4	*naalu*	17	*pathinezhu*
5	*anchu*	18	*pathinettu*
6	*aaru*	19	*paththonpathu*
7	*ezhu*	20	*irupathu*
8	*ettu*	100	*nooru*
9	*onpathu*	200	*irunnooru*
10	*paththu*	1000	*aayiram*
11	*pathinonnu*	2000	*randaayiram*
12	*panthrandu*	100,000	*laksham*
13	*pathimoonnu*		

Basic vocabulary

big	*valiya*	open	*thuranna*
small	*cheriya*	police station	*police station*
chemist	*marunnu kada*	road	*road*
clean	*vrithi ulla*	room	*room*
closed	*adachu*	shop	*kada*
cold	*thanuppulla*	sick (ill)	*asukham*
day	*divasam*	silk	*pattu*
dirty	*vrithi illaththa*	that	*athu*
English	*english*	this	*ithu*
excellent	*ugran*	town	*pattanam*
food/to eat	*aahaaram*	water	*vallam*
hot (spicy)	*erivulla*	what	*enthu*
hot (temp)	*choodulla*	when	*eppol*
luggage	*saadhanam*	where	*evide*
medicine	*marunnu*	which	*ethu*
newspaper	*dhinappathram*	who	*aaru*
of course, sure	*theerchayaayum*	why	*enthu kondu*

Food and drink

please show the menu	*menu kaanikkamo?*
no chillies please	*dhayavaayi mulaku idaruthu*
sugar/milk/ice	*panchasaara/paal/ice*
a bottle of water please	*oru kuppi vellam tharumo*
sweet/savoury	*madhuramulla/ruchiyulla*
spoon, fork, knife	*spoon, fork, kaththi*
chicken	*kozhiyirachi/chicken*
fish	*meen*
meat	*irachi*
prawns	*konchu/chemmeen*
vegetables	*pachakkari*
aubergine	*vazhuthina*
cabbage	*cabbage*
carrots	*carrot*
cauliflower	*cauliflower*
mushroom	*koon*
onion	*savaala*
okra, ladies'fingers	*vendacka*
peas	*payar*
potato	*urulakkizhangu*
spinach	*cheera*
plain boiled rice	*champaavari choru*

Index

Titles available in the Footprint *Focus* range

Latin America	UK RRP	US RRP
Bahia & Salvador	£7.99	$11.95
Brazilian Amazon	£7.99	$11.95
Brazilian Pantanal	£6.99	$9.95
Buenos Aires & Pampas	£7.99	$11.95
Cartagena & Caribbean Coast	£7.99	$11.95
Costa Rica	£8.99	$12.95
Cuzco, La Paz & Lake Titicaca	£8.99	$12.95
El Salvador	£5.99	$8.95
Guadalajara & Pacific Coast	£6.99	$9.95
Guatemala	£8.99	$12.95
Guyana, Guyane & Suriname	£5.99	$8.95
Havana	£6.99	$9.95
Honduras	£7.99	$11.95
Nicaragua	£7.99	$11.95
Northeast Argentina & Uruguay	£8.99	$12.95
Paraguay	£5.99	$8.95
Quito & Galápagos Islands	£7.99	$11.95
Recife & Northeast Brazil	£7.99	$11.95
Rio de Janeiro	£8.99	$12.95
São Paulo	£5.99	$8.95
Uruguay	£6.99	$9.95
Venezuela	£8.99	$12.95
Yucatán Peninsula	£6.99	$9.95

Asia	UK RRP	US RRP
Angkor Wat	£5.99	$8.95
Bali & Lombok	£8.99	$12.95
Chennai & Tamil Nadu	£8.99	$12.95
Chiang Mai & Northern Thailand	£7.99	$11.95
Goa	£6.99	$9.95
Gulf of Thailand	£8.99	$12.95
Hanoi & Northern Vietnam	£8.99	$12.95
Ho Chi Minh City & Mekong Delta	£7.99	$11.95
Java	£7.99	$11.95
Kerala	£7.99	$11.95
Kolkata & West Bengal	£5.99	$8.95
Mumbai & Gujarat	£8.99	$12.95

Africa & Middle East	UK RRP	US RRP
Beirut	£6.99	$9.95
Cairo & Nile Delta	£8.99	$12.95
Damascus	£5.99	$8.95
Durban & KwaZulu Natal	£8.99	$12.95
Fès & Northern Morocco	£8.99	$12.95
Jerusalem	£8.99	$12.95
Johannesburg & Kruger National Park	£7.99	$11.95
Kenya's Beaches	£8.99	$12.95
Kilimanjaro & Northern Tanzania	£8.99	$12.95
Luxor to Aswan	£8.99	$12.95
Nairobi & Rift Valley	£7.99	$11.95
Red Sea & Sinai	£7.99	$11.95
Zanzibar & Pemba	£7.99	$11.95

Europe	UK RRP	US RRP
Bilbao & Basque Region	£6.99	$9.95
Brittany West Coast	£7.99	$11.95
Cádiz & Costa de la Luz	£6.99	$9.95
Granada & Sierra Nevada	£6.99	$9.95
Languedoc: Carcassonne to Montpellier	£7.99	$11.95
Málaga	£5.99	$8.95
Marseille & Western Provence	£7.99	$11.95
Orkney & Shetland Islands	£5.99	$8.95
Santander & Picos de Europa	£7.99	$11.95
Sardinia: Alghero & the North	£7.99	$11.95
Sardinia: Cagliari & the South	£7.99	$11.95
Seville	£5.99	$8.95
Sicily: Palermo & the Northwest	£7.99	$11.95
Sicily: Catania & the Southeast	£7.99	$11.95
Siena & Southern Tuscany	£7.99	$11.95
Sorrento, Capri & Amalfi Coast	£6.99	$9.95
Skye & Outer Hebrides	£6.99	$9.95
Verona & Lake Garda	£7.99	$11.95

North America	UK RRP	US RRP
Vancouver & Rockies	£8.99	$12.95

Australasia	UK RRP	US RRP
Brisbane & Queensland	£8.99	$12.95
Perth	£7.99	$11.95

For the latest books, e-books and a wealth of travel information, visit us at:
www.footprinttravelguides.com.

Join us on facebook for the latest travel news, product releases, offers and amazing competitions:
www.facebook.com/footprintbooks.